T0318144

DAVIDE MACULLO ARCHITECTS
JANSEN CAMPUS

DAVIDE MACULLO ARCHITECTS
JANSEN CAMPUS

SKIRA

Cover
Photo by Enrico Cano, Como

Back Cover
Sketch by Davide Macullo Architects, Lugano

Design
Marcello Francone

Editorial Coordination
Vincenza Russo

Editorial Assistance
Lorenza Tallarini, Davide Macullo Architects, Lugano

Editing
Domenico Pertocoli

Layout
Paola Ranzini
Davide Macullo Architects

Translations
Aileen Forbes-Munnelly, Davide Macullo Architects, Lugano
Dogrel AG, Widnau

Photocredits
Pino Musi, Milan, Italy: 10, 42, 44, 46, 48, 60, 61, 62, 63, 64, 70, 72
centre and right, 73, 76, 77, 78, 79, 80, 84, 90, 95, 96, 97, 100, 101, 102,
104, 106, 107, 109, 112, 113, 114, 115 left bottom and right top, 132
Enrico Cano, Como, Italy: cover, 20, 50, 52, 65, 72 left top and left
bottom, 74, 85, 88, 92, 94, 98, 103, 115 left top and right bottom,
122, 138
Davide Macullo Architects: 6, 12, 66, 118, 142

First published in Italy in 2013 by
Skira Editore S.p.A.
Palazzo Casati Stampa
via Torino 61
20123 Milano
Italy
www.skira.net

© 2013 by Davide Macullo Architects
© 2013 Skira editore

Printed and bound in Italy. First edition

ISBN: 978-88-572-1866-3

Pages 6-7
View of the Rheintal region (spring)

Contents

The making of a vision

9   Foreword
Gabriele Cappellato

14   Drawing from context
Davide Macullo

17   Jansen. Oberriet. Rheintal. Switzerland. Europe. The World
Kuno Bont

25   Sensual pragmatism: building a vision
Davide Macullo

27   Aligning Nature & Future: the Jansen Art Collection
Sophia Hyoseon Kim

117   Family values
Priska & Christoph Jansen

124   Fact sheet

127   Buildings and projects

135   Publications

140   Aknowledgements

141   Biographical notes

THE MAKING OF A VISION

Gabriele Cappellato

Foreword

Good architecture, set in context, becomes a place. For Le Corbusier this is key to his reflections and convictions: there is a very close relationship between architecture and context. The same concept of context prefigures conditions of light, air and landscape; the fundamental elements needed for the preservation of the existing balance between nature and architecture. The physical context of a project is represented by these elements that make up the natural landscape. Under this premise, Davide Macullo's project for the Jansen Campus is set in Oberriet, a small nucleus in the Rhine Valley that, along with the Vorarlberg represents one of the most industrialised areas in Switzerland.

This village is typified by a multitude of different sized inclined planes, sloping in different directions. It is the sloping roofs that create a vibrant effect of light and shade throughout the day that characterise the built space of this place. The facades of the buildings appear to lose their importance, assuming the supportive roles of the great inclined plans. The new geometry of the building has been generated by this complexity of the "game of planes".

The site for the construction of the new Jansen Campus lies at the north end of the industrial complex and is bordered by the more fragmented residential fabric of the village. This particular site allows the new building to insert itself as the link between two different urban scales, acting as the face of the industrial area while also reducing to the scale of the village.

The new building was preceded by a masterplan of the Jansen site, resulting from the necessary expansion of existing industrial structures and which then allowed for the creation of spaces on a human scale within the existing fabric. This has led to the formation of a series of spaces that evoke the atmosphere of public squares. The project, during its phases of construction has been transformed into a reality that has assumed regional importance, destined to create attention also at national and international level.

The building develops around a succession of four volumes, set in a triangular plan. These elements are modelled according to their relationship to the surrounding landscape, in such a way as to underline a dynamic idea of collective function, mirroring the company's social principles of work.

Building on the client's own commitment to the sustainable management of its production and logistics and in keeping with the company's ethics and technical excellence in this field, the building meets the exacting Minergie standards, with the aim of improving the quality of life of its users, efficient energy use, reducing environmental impact and a competitiveness in maintenance costs. Throughout the design of the project, there was interesting and specific research carried out in the use of innovative materials and technological solutions, some of which were used for the first time in the construction industry. Jansen Campus was realised taking advantage of the resources available in the surrounding area, showing the high level of entrepreneurship in the region and the attention given to collective efficient and real energy savings.

The internal landscape is articulated as a fluid space, almost as if it were formed by an extension of the collective spaces of the surrounding urban fabric. A new landscape is created, a system of solids and voids expanding in all directions. The apparent mass of the new building is dematerialised internally, flooded with natural light teeming through the generous openings and grand slicing overhangs that project the users out to the landscape. The building also draws from the extraordinary beauty of its natural surroundings and recreates part of this external atmosphere within its own internal landscape.

Architecture, with respect to the place in which it is set, establishes a dialectic relationship because it enters into the process of the continual transformation of the landscape and the territory due to the passing of time. This relationship with the context affords architecture the principle of the modification of the anthropic space that defines the identity of a place. Identity, understood as recognition, is fundamental component for a good architectural a project and this contributes to the realisation of an artefact of quality.

This architectural project is understood not only as a creative act, ruled by the techniques of control and manipulation of space, but it also corresponds to the significant potential of the existing physical, historical and cultural reality.

Davide Macullo

Drawing from context

A competitive industry in the global marketplace must continually reinvent itself and show a strong character while still remaining adaptable to the changing conditions of the world stage. This condition is a fundamental element of the approach to building a place that is to become the physical representation of a company. Just like the quality of a person, the urbanism and architecture are born out of the attention and care for details and the search for harmony between elements.

The facade is clad in a dark prepatinated perforated Rheinzink mesh. This particular finish gives the material a colouring that evokes the density of the tones of the wooden buildings of the surrounding area. Used for the first time as an external cladding, this "skin" has the particular quality of making the building seem "light". The facade shimmers with reflections and shadows, changing throughout the day, with the changing of the hour and the light of the day; a constant dialogue between the material, light, the environment and the elements. It is hard to find the same conditions twice. The density of the mesh, the dimensions of the panels, the distance of the fixings from the wind protection layer – all contribute to giving an appearance of three-dimensionality to the facade. The modular design and the tight stretched mesh play a role in the scale of the building and make it interesting for approaching visitors.

The new Jansen Campus is also characterised by research, carried out during the design, on innovative materials and technological solutions – some used for the first time in construction. For example the semi-structural facade, produced by Jansen, is a new system produced in such a way as to guarantee a continuity of the reflective, glazed and transparent elements of the building without the need for external support mechanisms.

In order to build the sloping roofs of the building, a system of adding fibres to the concrete casting was developed. Doing this guaranteed that the poured cement would adhere to the metal reinforcements. An innovative radiant system (TABS), partly produced by Jansen, based on thermal mass principles, has also been integrated into the structure; heating and cooling circuits have been installed directly into the concrete structure forming the floors and ceilings, ensuring the quality conditioning of all spaces.

Despite its sophistication, the atmosphere of the internal landscape reflects the principle of reducing details to a minimum. The constructive elements are therefore always explicit and follow the rationale and economy of the site and the project, giving the space a technical, industrial atmosphere.

The suspended ceiling required a long planning process and considerable effort by those specialists involved. The technological elements – the ventilation, audio, sound absorption, lighting motion and smoke detection systems – were condensed with great precision within one sculptural element that runs through the spaces and accompanies users about the building. These ceilings along with their decorative function, emphasise the meaning of the space. Two versions were designed, depending on the height of the space in which they are located. Compared to a traditional fully suspended ceiling covering the entire roof area, this solution meets the same functions yet it is more economical. In addition, the materiality of the ceilings, through the interlaced layers of mesh and light, has an increased effect on the perception of the space and its three-dimensionality.

The white RAL 9016 used as a base colour throughout the building was chosen for its neutral characteristics and to accommodate the designers' wishes to create a colourful, warm internal landscape without creating an emotional tension for the users. This may seem contradictory; however, through the expedient and daring use of colour on concealed surfaces, the Campus offers a welcoming and warm atmosphere. The building is alive with hidden colour; coloured elements peek out from behind the perforated metal of the office furniture, from the acoustic panels of the walls and ceilings, behind sand blasted glass, and from brightly painted niches reflections and shadows of colour emerge indirectly. At the same time, other areas of the building were deliberately coloured and provide an ulterior reading of the internal landscape. These three-dimensional abstract surfaces are not simply physical walls but serve as mnemonic reminders that accompany users throughout the building, creating a sense of belonging in this internal composition. The illumination of the intercoms for the individual office entrance doors are a further reduction of scale of the building. Through the spatial administration of these repetitive elements at different scales, and through the careful and playful choice of furnishings, the individual takes on a sense of

orientation and safety. Perception is stimulated continuously, but in a harmonious way.

Art works chosen for the building are by international contemporary artists, as the same generation of the clients and architects, realised within the past three years (the period corresponding to the design and construction of the Jansen Campus) and have a connection to the theme "nature and technology"; nature to bring primordial inspiration into industry; technology as an affinity for the effort in creating new technologies that echo the company's philosophy.

Pages 18-19
Swiss national map extract

Pages 20-21
Aerial view
The Campus acts as a link
between the industry
and the village of Oberriet

Pages 22-23
Davide Macullo's *Iscape* (detail)

Kuno Bont

Jansen. Oberriet. Rheintal. Switzerland. Europe. The World

I had just become a real first-year primary school pupil – proud of my new cowhide-covered school satchel, which I always carried with me – when I had the following experience in my father's barber's shop: "The man works at Jansens", explained my father in his thick Swiss-German dialect, while his scissors made a continuously snip-snip noise and the man's severed grey hair began to cover the floor like a light snow shower. My father, the barber, in his white barber's jacket, combed the man's hair back uncompromisingly with Brylcreem, while holding the nimbly opening and closing hairdresser's scissors in his right hand: a picture of a barber. I, the little lad, sitting on one of the yellow chairs, where usually only men sat and waited until their turn came. A picture of a really small kid, who had just begun to discover the world of adults. Directly in front of the big mirror in the salon, at least half of him hidden under a wide blue cape, sat the man who worked at Jansens: a short, generally upwardly shaped haircut, a stubbly beard, hands bearing the marks of work and grease, blue overtrousers, a jacket in the same blue with slightly too short sleeves and a furrowed, friendly face. A picture of a worker, which I can still call to mind today, when I need a truly typical worker for my films or photographs.

The man came directly off his shift to the barber and enjoyed the opportunity of sitting in the upholstered chair for a while. Tomorrow his daughter would be married, he had therefore been given the day off by his boss. I was to find all this out bit by bit. A lot of talking goes on in the barber's chair. But soon the shave and hair-

cut were over. The haircut took ten minutes or so, the shave about five, then my father held the mirror up to the man who worked at Jansens and proudly showed him his work from all sides and from all angles. With an elegant movement, he whisked off the gown, the sturdily built man stood up and reached into his back trouser pocket with his hand to take out a flattened wallet. Then I saw it: the blue lettering on the breast pocket of his overall. I read "J... Ja... Jan... sen". And from then on I also wanted to be a man in the factory at Jansens.

Many years have passed since then. Progress has made its mark in the village. I didn't become a worker at Jansens, instead I became a politician, journalist and film-maker. Oberriet has long since given up its ranking as the longest street village in Switzerland, a fact which was always being driven into us as schoolchildren. The village in which for a while one in every seven of its working population was employed at Jansen, has not stood still. The girls, who were once taught upstairs in the town hall separately from the boys, have long since been brought out of their isolation and returned to mixed-gender classes. We had some wild times, and I was certainly not one of the most well-behaved pupils. In spite of that I managed to learn something at the town hall. I met a lot of people from Jansen there. And there I first became aware of what it meant when someone says: "He works at Jansens." He was not referring to a company, he meant a family. That's Jansen.

No-one could hold a candle to the doyen of industrialisation in the village when it came to continu-

ous development. To the steel tubes were soon added plastic pipes, then window profiles, and most recently the renowned company expanded with large new buildings on the other side of the railway line and into the wide world. Jansen provided economic buoyancy to the community and offered secure jobs. And today, people still like to work at Jansen. Because at Jansen there is no place for extreme risk, and there never was.

Jansen is also typically Rheintal. Chancental. Pioneering spirit. Endurance. Diligence. These are Rheintal characteristics, deeply rooted in the people, the landscape, the sparse moorland and the splendid surrounding mountains. And it is this very panorama that Davide Macullo took up in the remarkable architectural signature of the newly erected Jansen Campus. Viewed from a distance, the fascinating building with its peaked roofs stretches upwards like a new plant caught springing out of the earth and reaching for the sky. Breaking through resistance, looking to progress, steeped in stability and steadfastness, with just the right amount of excitement, but based firmly on solid ground. The naturalness, which is readily evident to the viewer, is not forced and fits perfectly with the company's image today, a globally active organisation with an immense ability to innovate. Jansen. Oberriet. Rheintal. Switzerland. Europe. The World.

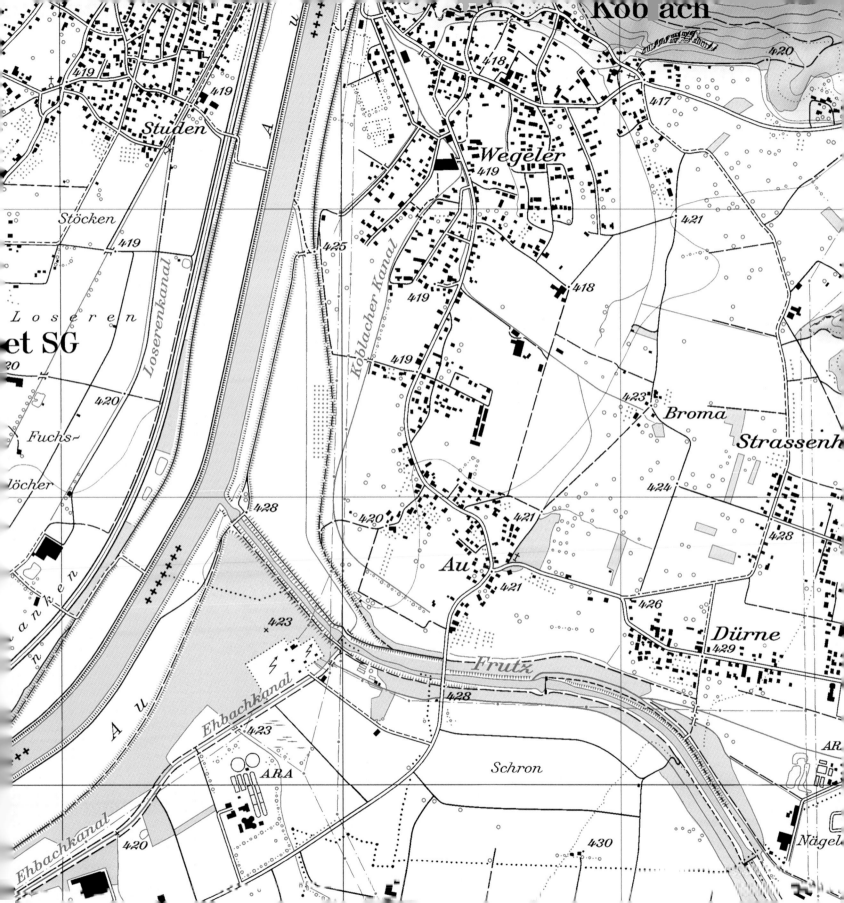

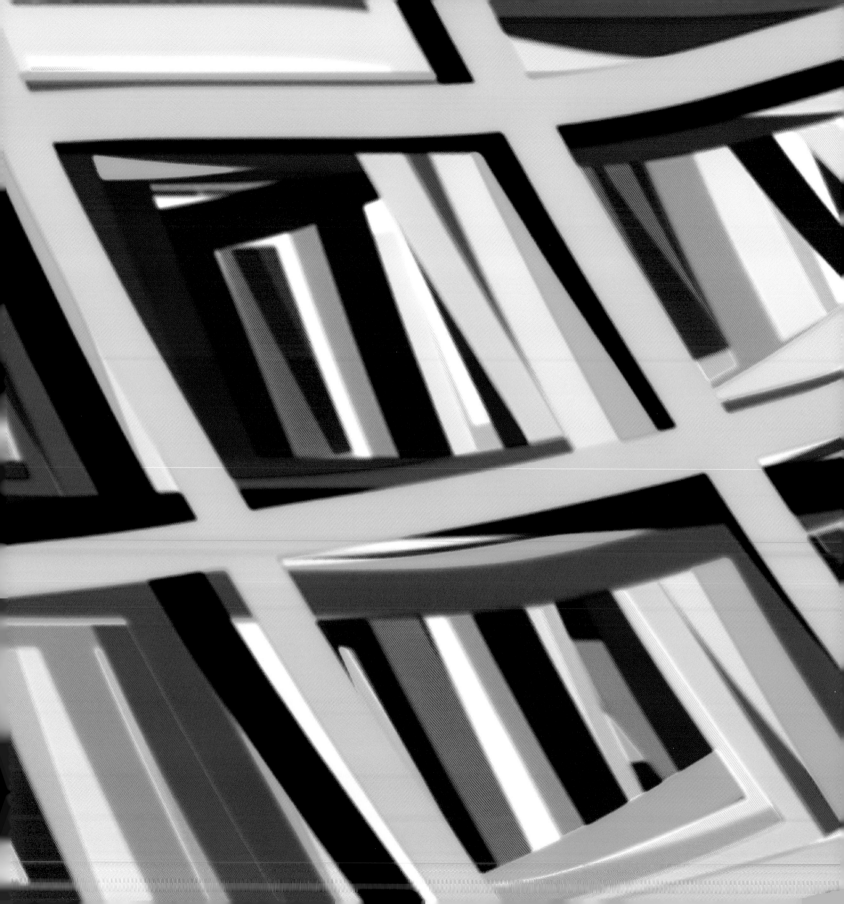

Davide Macullo

Sensual pragmatism: building a vision

The landscape of the plains of the Rhine Valley evokes the image of an era once dominated by endless glaciers. Even today it has a particular beauty; in the morning when the sky merges with the frost-covered hills and fields, there is an alienating feeling of lightness, almost a loss of a sense of gravity. This is a land that speaks of ancient navigators of the Rhine, of the industriousness of the first settlements, built to withstand the harsh and complex territory. It is a place that speaks of the history of a people who have had to put ethics before aesthetics for survival. It is these echoes of the past and the shades of the landscape that inform the volumes and principles of the new Jansen Campus.

The built form is reminiscent of a ship stranded amongst the glaciers of the Rhine. The emerging elements appear to adopt the form of old existing buildings and it is as if the new presence is formed in part by an original settlement. Its primaeval foundations help crystallise its contemporary relevance. The volumes align themselves to form a new landscape that reacts, through its forms and the use of technology, to the climatic variations.

A condition of nature becomes one of culture, projecting man along a journey of the senses and the mind towards an inner ambition to harness his creative potential. The expressiveness pursued in the design of this place is based on the emotions of those who live there. Before revealing its rationale, a work of architecture is built around the perception of the individual.

The great challenge of contemporary architecture lies in the exaltation of the quality of life of residents through the harmony of built spaces, reducing the representation of hierarchies bound to the past. The ability of contemporary design, liberated from the dogmas of the past, is in the strength to return to the essentiality of human needs, implementing a design that works on emotions that are stimulated as one approaches the place. The architecture is, from afar, a form and therefore a sign of expression in the existing context; close up it becomes a collection of many things, where the scale of perception begins to welcome the individual, and from within, it is a world in which man finds the stimuli and harmony to cultivate his visions.

By delving into the roots of the place and investigating its future needs, both known and unknown, architecture acts as the bridge between the DNA of a place and its future.

Davide Macullo's *Iscape*

Sophia Hyoseon Kim

Curator of the Collection

Aligning Nature & Future: the Jansen Art Collection

A corporate art collection can be thought of as a path through which corporate staff are encouraged to visit the cultural world based upon accessibility rather than on the basis of metaphysical interpretations that assume a high cultural taste and context. Consequently, the art collection of Jansen takes this concept very much to heart and is organised under the theme Nature and Future. These themes are intimately connected to the project as a whole.

Nature in this collection refers to the modern concept of "nature" governed by the environment and civilization rather than its classic concept. The *future* element of the collection takes its inspiration from the combination of architecture and industry. Here, the architecture of the new building represents the solidity of the Jansen family business, but also projects it into the future and there is a certain elasticity among the works present in the collection that responds to and reflects this.

The marriage of the aesthetic nature of the two subjects is what gives the collection its sense of harmony. Rather than each individual work existing solely within its own specific frame of reference, as part of a collective, they offer together a different perspective. The ethos is inclusive and these mutual strands of nature and future, of hope and possibility, are communicated across the collection. The cohort of international artists included offers its contemporary view of the world and the hope is that the contemporaneity of these artists and their work will be read in parallel to that of the corporate world within which they reside.

We hope that the works installed throughout the lobby and hallways, offices, conference rooms and lounges of Jansen's new office building provide the company's staff with a sense of peace and day-to-day well-being and will, at the same time, provide Jansen with the additional energy required to create an exciting and innovative artistic space.

Pages 28-35
Study sketches

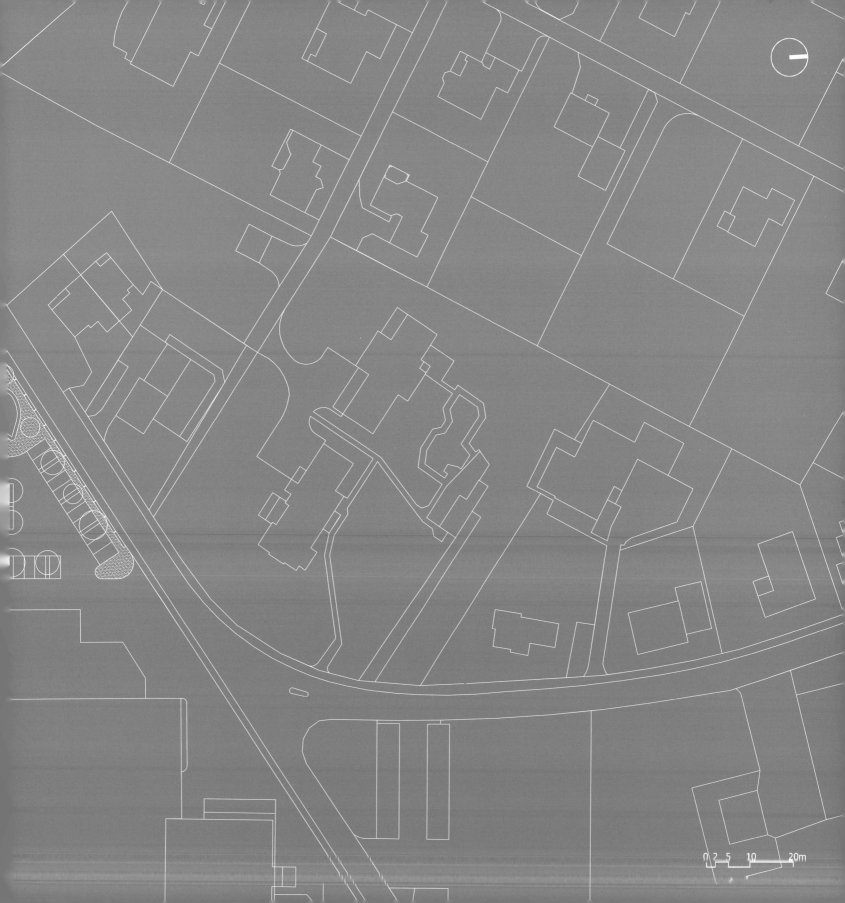

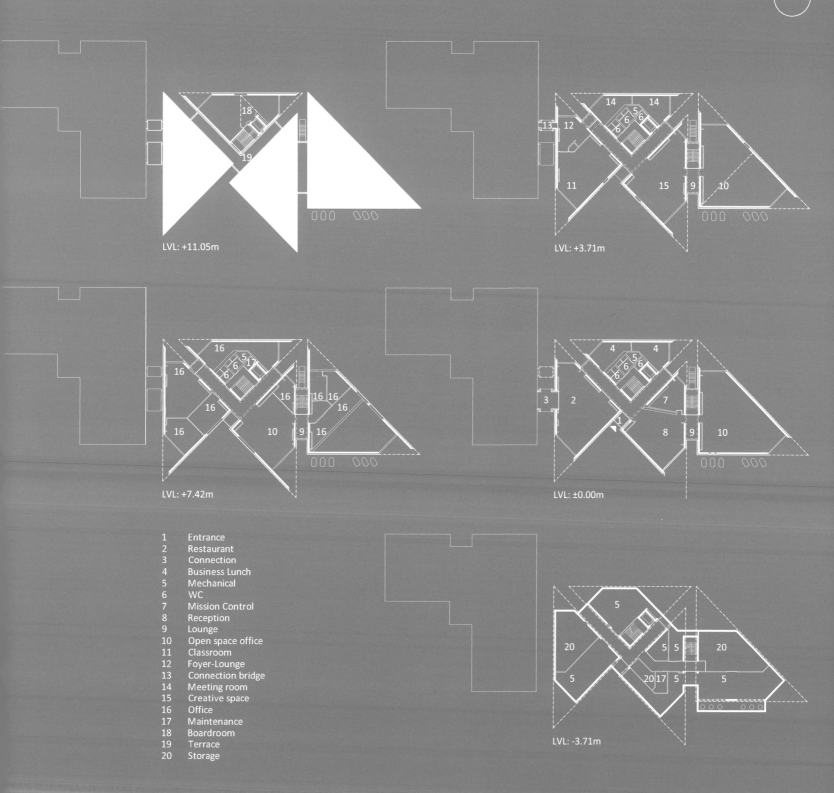

LVL: +11.05m

LVL: +3.71m

LVL: +7.42m

LVL: ±0.00m

LVL: -3.71m

1	Entrance
2	Restaurant
3	Connection
4	Business Lunch
5	Mechanical
6	WC
7	Mission Control
8	Reception
9	Lounge
10	Open space office
11	Classroom
12	Foyer-Lounge
13	Connection bridge
14	Meeting room
15	Creative space
16	Office
17	Maintenance
18	Boardroom
19	Terrace
20	Storage

0 2 5   10   20m

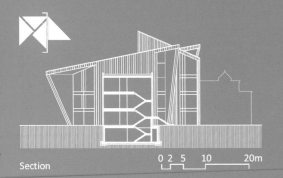

Section

0 2 5   10   20m

East view

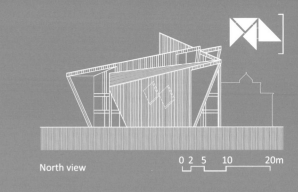
North view

0 2 5 10 20m

0 2 5 10m

Southeast view

Pages 50-51
Southeast night view

Pages 52-53
Detail of the *Rheinzink* mesh façade

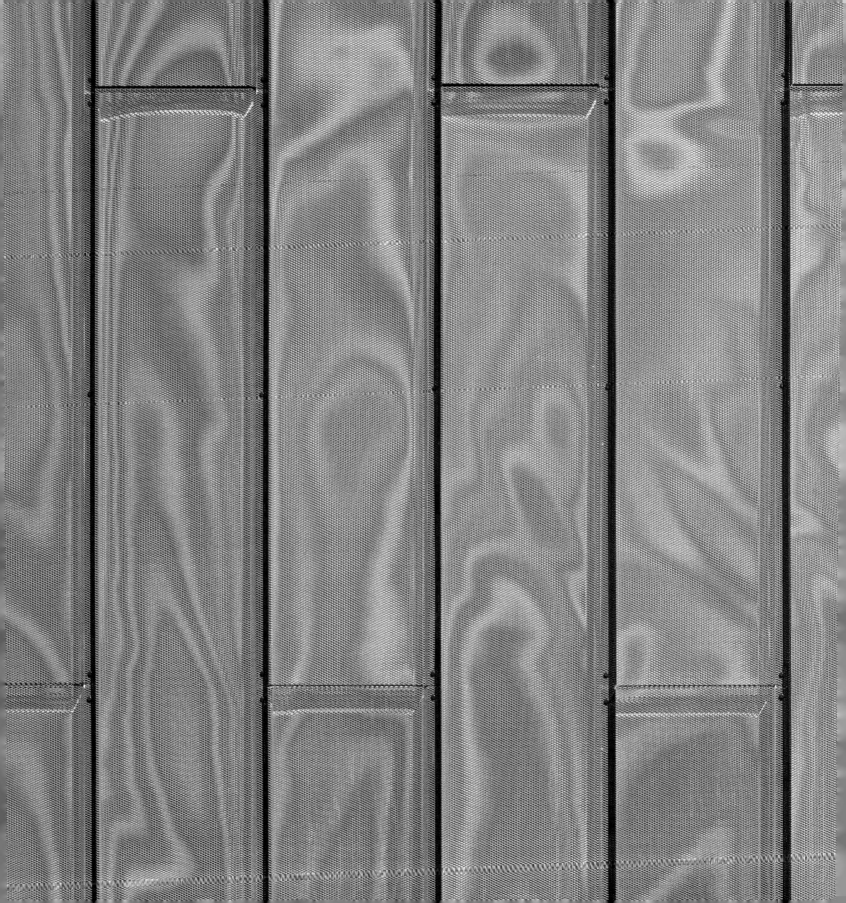

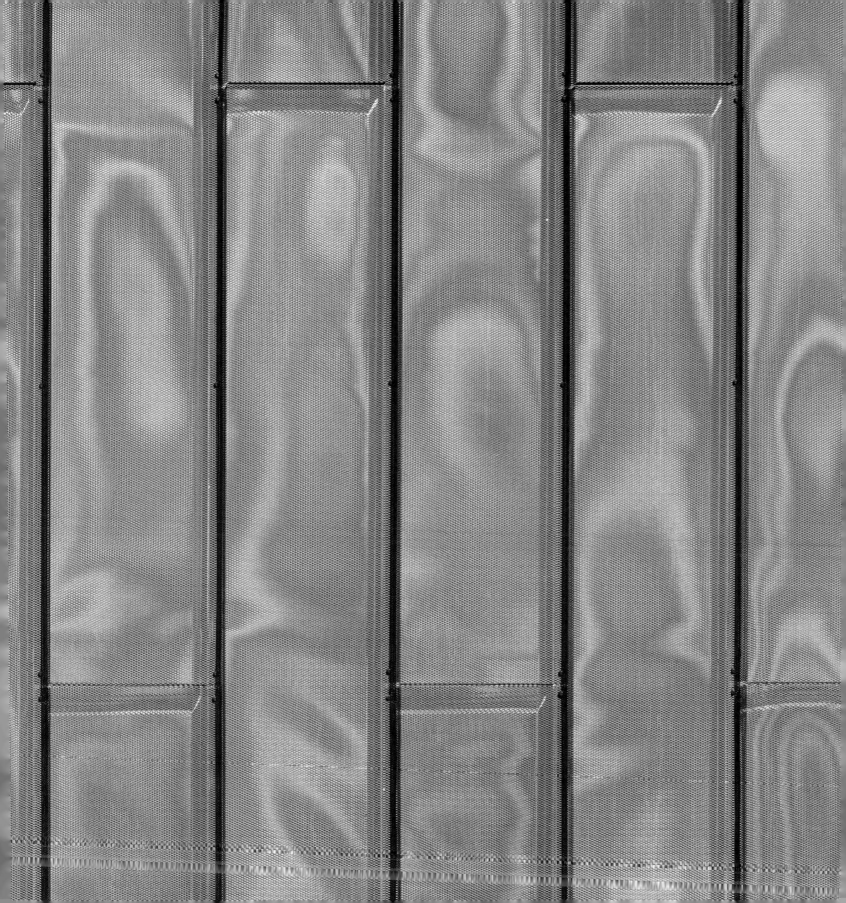

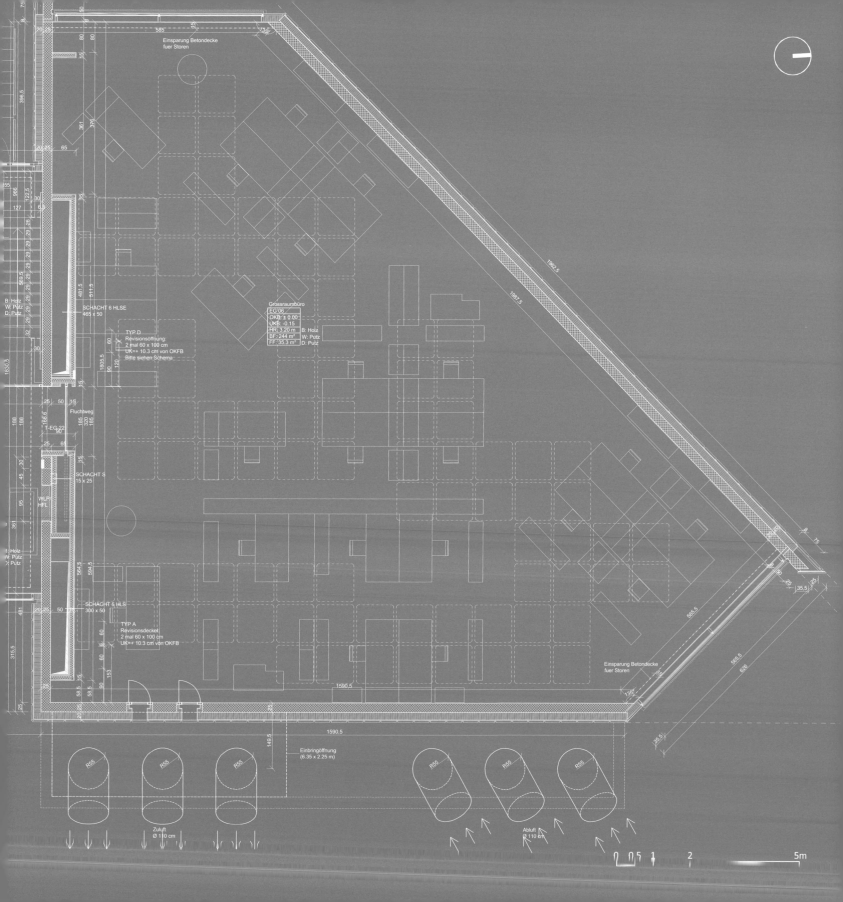

Einsparung Betondecke
fuer Storen

SCHACHT 6 HLSE
465 x 50

TYP D
Revisionsöffnung:
2 mal 60 x 100 cm
UK=+ 10.3 cm von OKFB
Bitte siehen Schema

Grossraumbüro
EG '06
OKB: ± 0.00
UKB: -0.15
HR: 3.20 m   B: Holz
BF: 244 m²   W: Putz
FF: 35.3 m²   D. Putz

B: Holz
W: Putz
D. Putz

Fluchtweg

T-EG 22

SCHACHT S
15 x 25

WLP/
HFL

Holz
Putz
Putz

SCHACHT 5 HLS
300 x 50

TYP A
Revisionsdeckel
2 mal 60 x 100 cm
UK=+ 10.3 cm von OKFB

1590,5

Einsparung Betondecke
fuer Storen

1590,5

Einbringöffnung
(6.35 x 2.25 m)

R55

R55

R55

R55

R55

R55

Zuluft
Ø 110 cm

Abluft
Ø 110 cm

5m

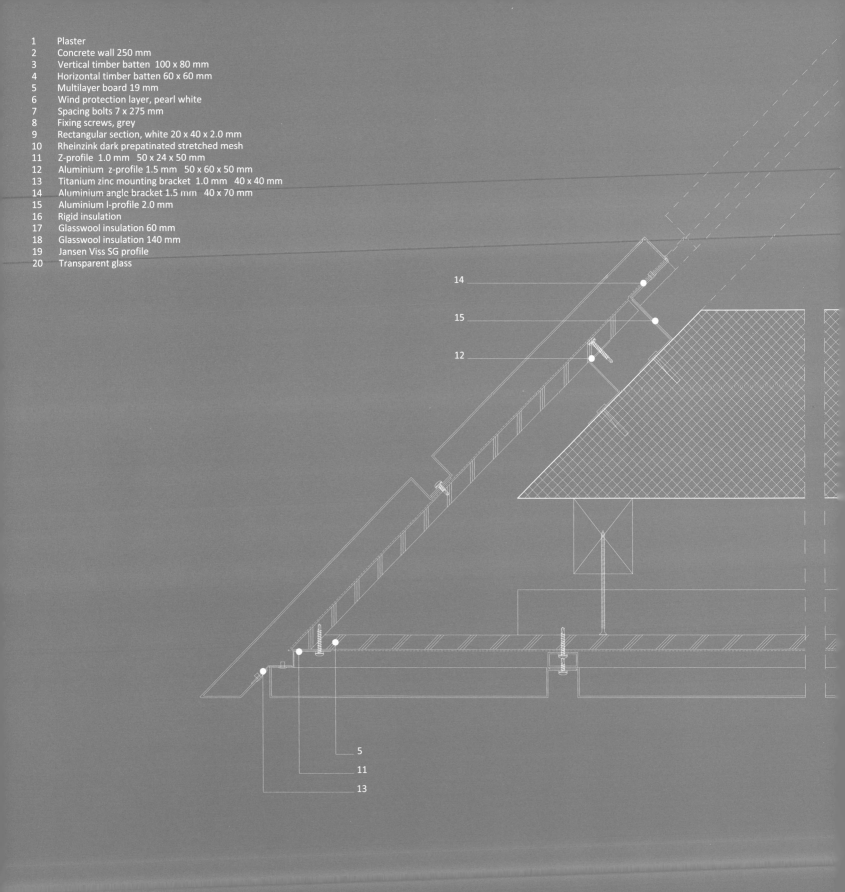

1 Plaster
2 Concrete wall 250 mm
3 Vertical timber batten 100 x 80 mm
4 Horizontal timber batten 60 x 60 mm
5 Multilayer board 19 mm
6 Wind protection layer, pearl white
7 Spacing bolts 7 x 275 mm
8 Fixing screws, grey
9 Rectangular section, white 20 x 40 x 2.0 mm
10 Rheinzink dark prepatinated stretched mesh
11 Z-profile 1.0 mm 50 x 24 x 50 mm
12 Aluminium z-profile 1.5 mm 50 x 60 x 50 mm
13 Titanium zinc mounting bracket 1.0 mm 40 x 40 mm
14 Aluminium anglc bracket 1.5 mm 40 x 70 mm
15 Aluminium l-profile 2.0 mm
16 Rigid insulation
17 Glasswool insulation 60 mm
18 Glasswool insulation 140 mm
19 Jansen Viss SG profile
20 Transparent glass

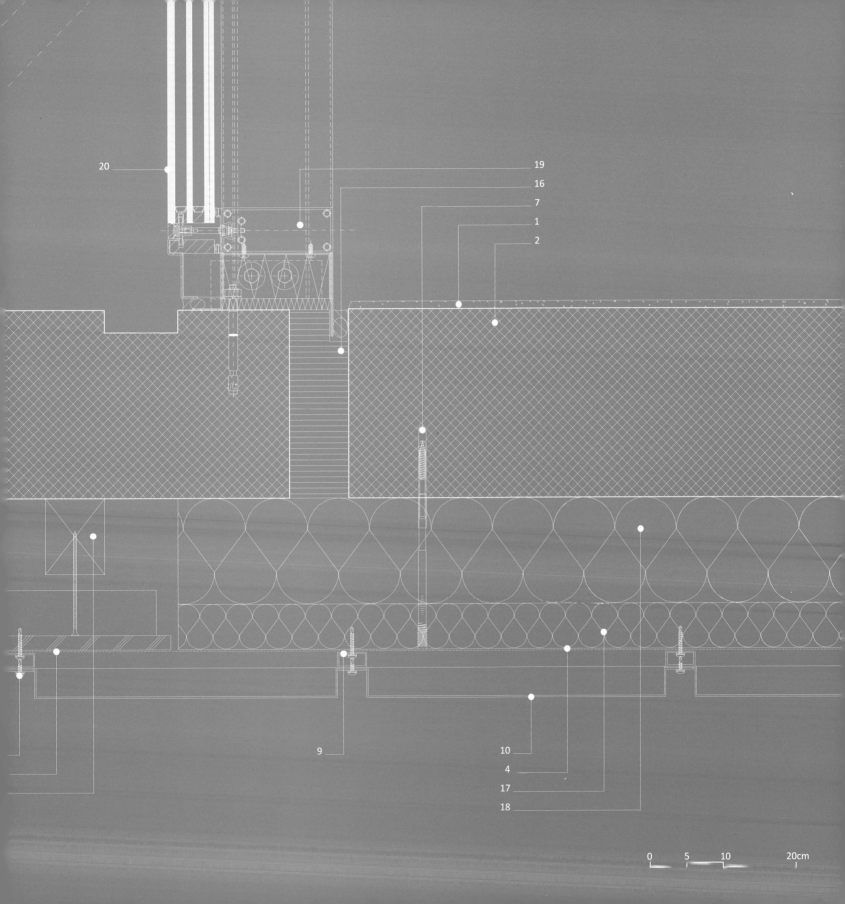

20

19

16

7

1

2

9

10

4

17

18

0   5   10   20cm

1   Plaster
2   Concrete wall 250 mm
4   Horizontal timber batten 60 x 60 mm
5   Multilayer board 19 mm
6   Wind protection layer, pearl white
7   Spacing bolts 7 x 275 mm
8   Fixing screws, grey
9   Rectangular section, white 20 x 40 x 2.0 mm
10   Rheinzink dark prepatinated stretched mesh
17   Glasswool insulation 60 mm
18   Glasswool insulation 140 mm
19   Jansen Viss SG profile
20   Transparent glass
21   Painted glass

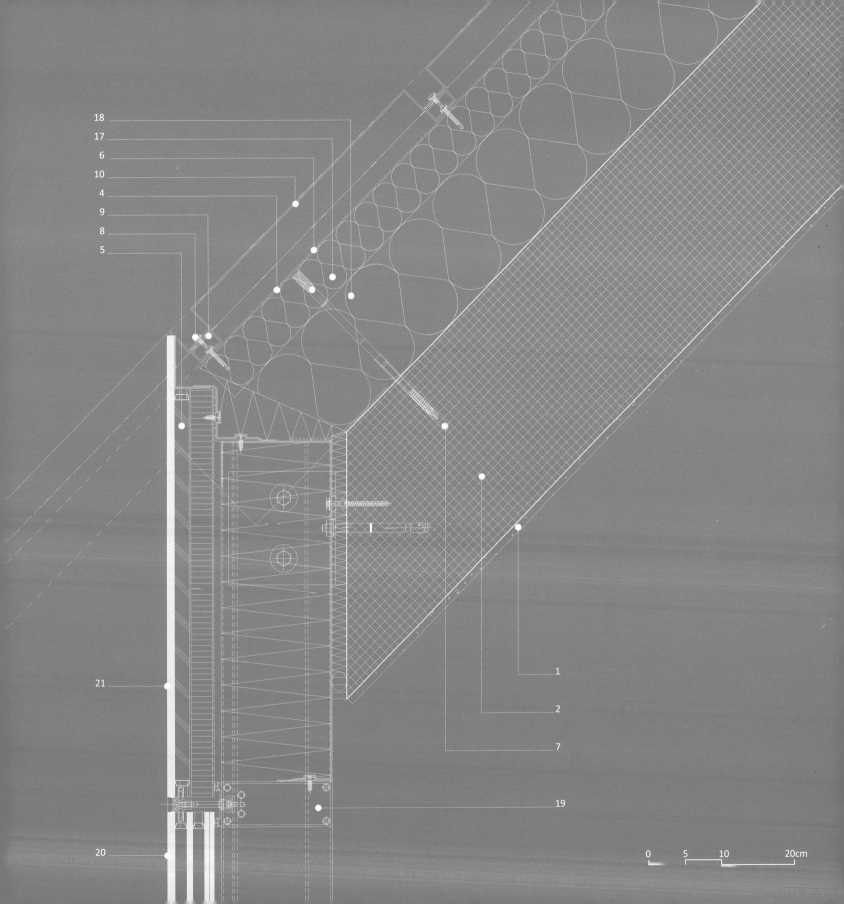

18

17

6

10

4

9

8

5

21

20

1

2

7

19

0   5   10   20cm

Left
Northwest view

Upper right
North view

Lower right
Curtain wall detail view

West night view (detail)

Pages 66-67
Landscape study sketches

Pages 70-71
Jansen Campus outdoor benches

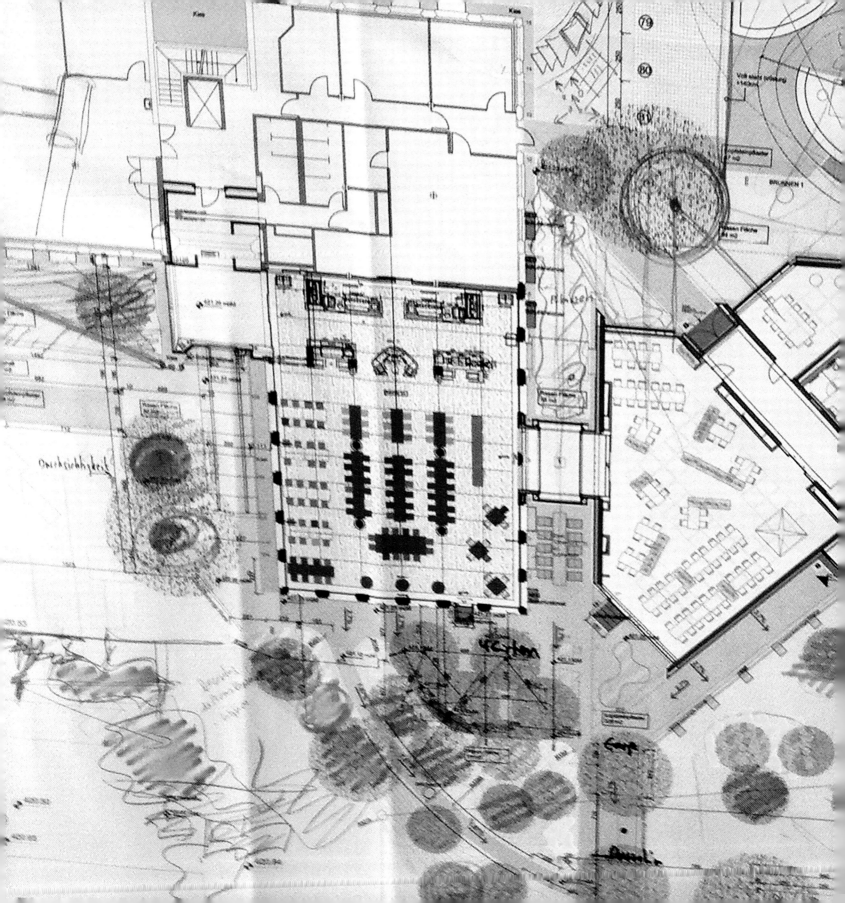

WASSE

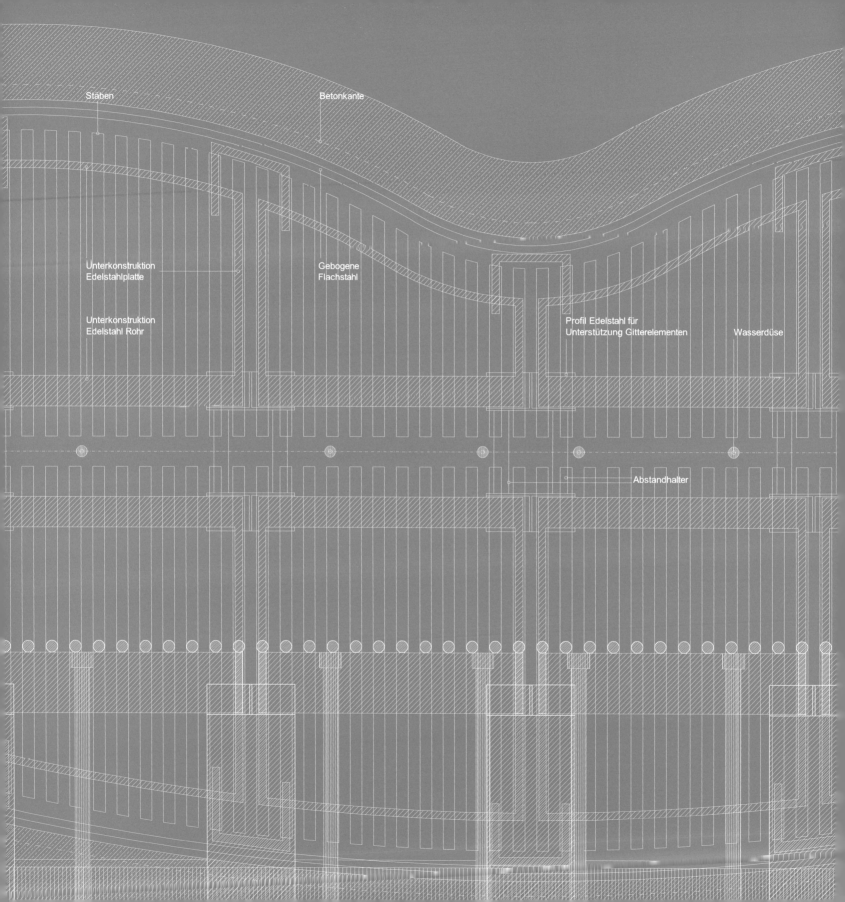

Stäben

Betonkante

Unterkonstruktion
Edelstahlplatte

Gebogene
Flachstahl

Unterkonstruktion
Edelstahl Rohr

Profil Edelstahl für
Unterstützung Gitterelementen

Wasserdüse

Abstandhalter

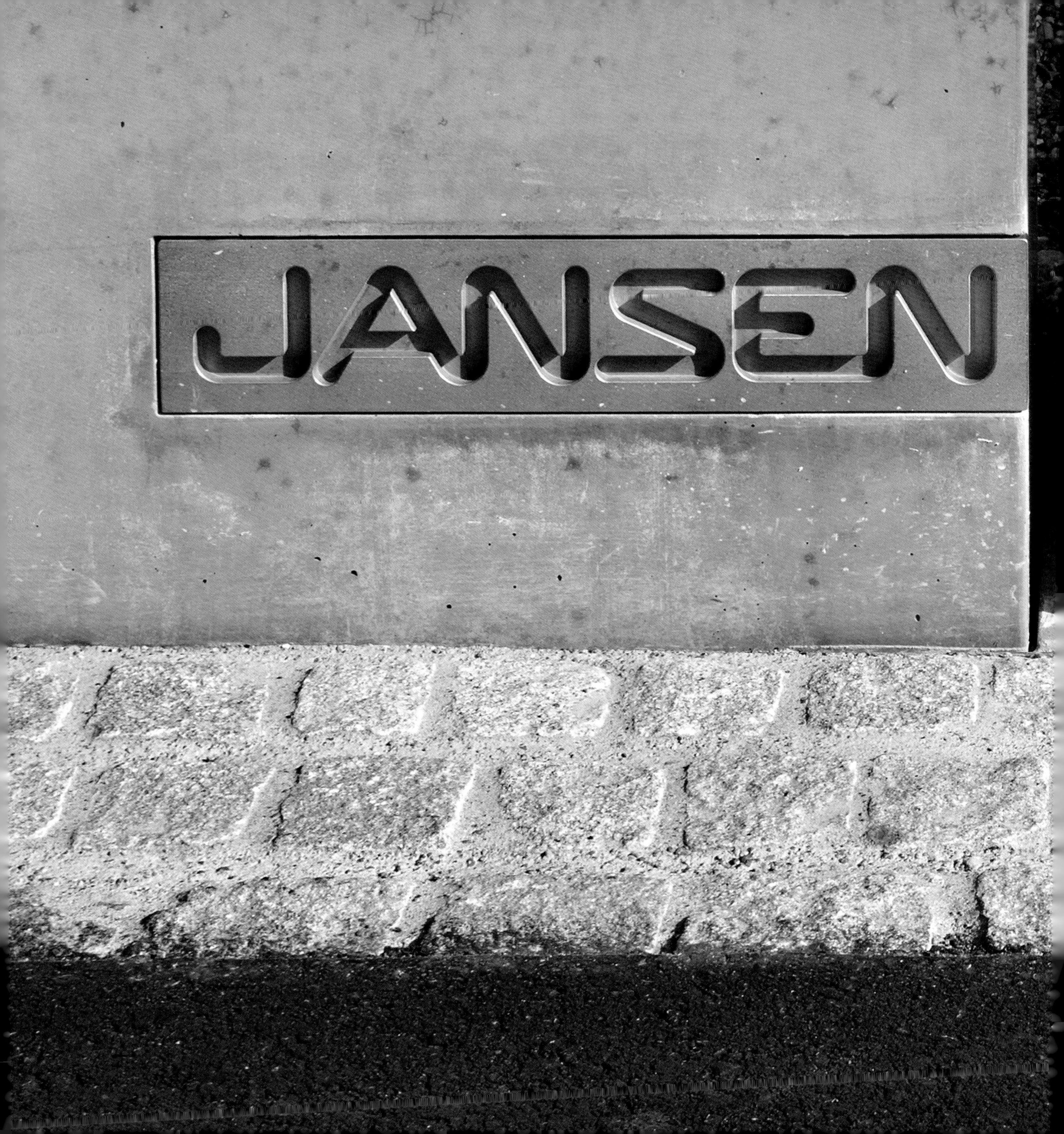
JANSEN

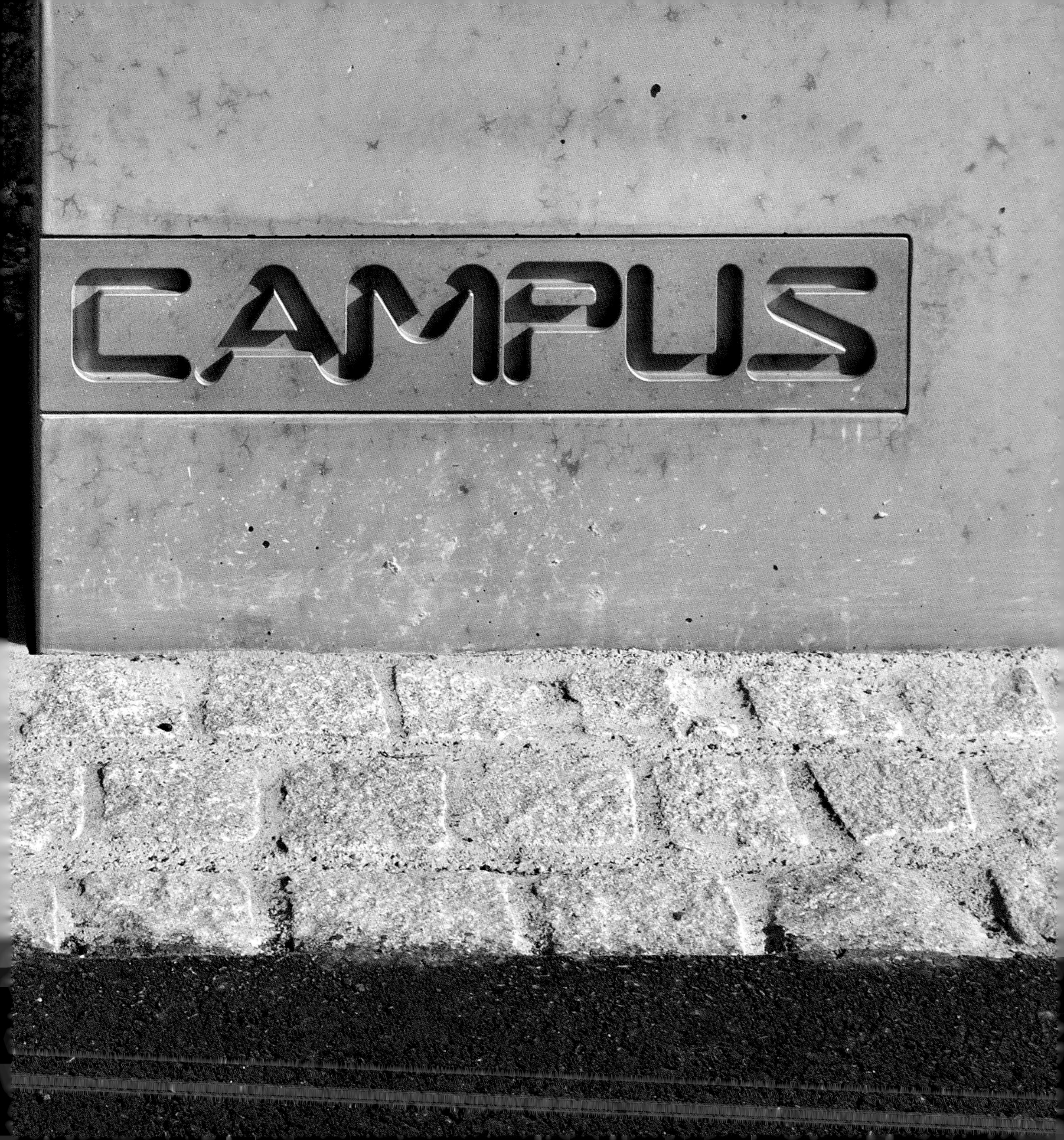
CAMPUS

Landscape design (fountain, granite
chair from the logo of the architect)

Opposite page
Entrance door

Pages 74-75
Detail view of the art work *Wallwave
Vibration* by Loris Cecchini

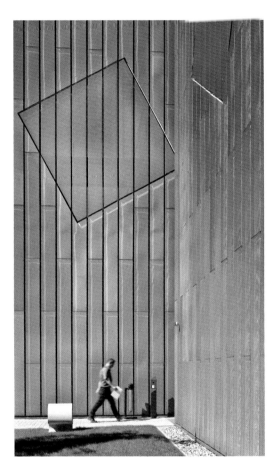

Lobby area with art work *Wallwave Vibration* by Loris Cecchini

Lobby area detail views with printed
study sketches on wall by the
architect for the Campus

Pages 80-81
Detail view of the suspended ceiling
in the staff restaurant

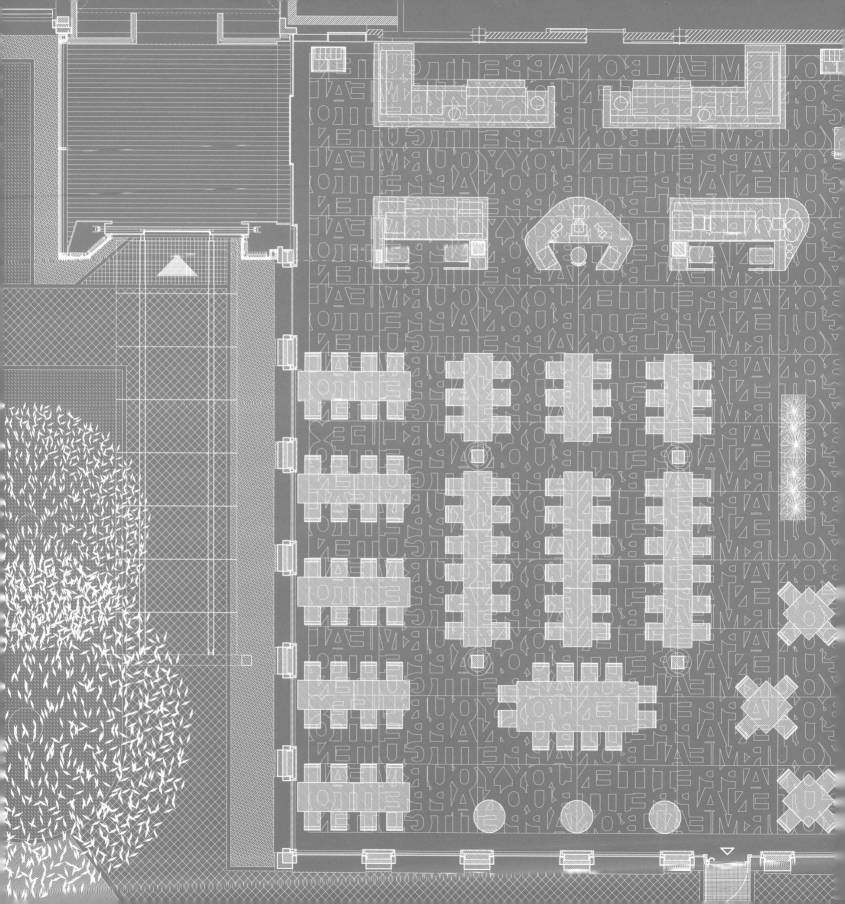

Interior views of the refurbishment
of the staff restaurant with
Davide Macullo's *Iscape* sketch

Pages 88-91
Suspended technical ceiling detail
views

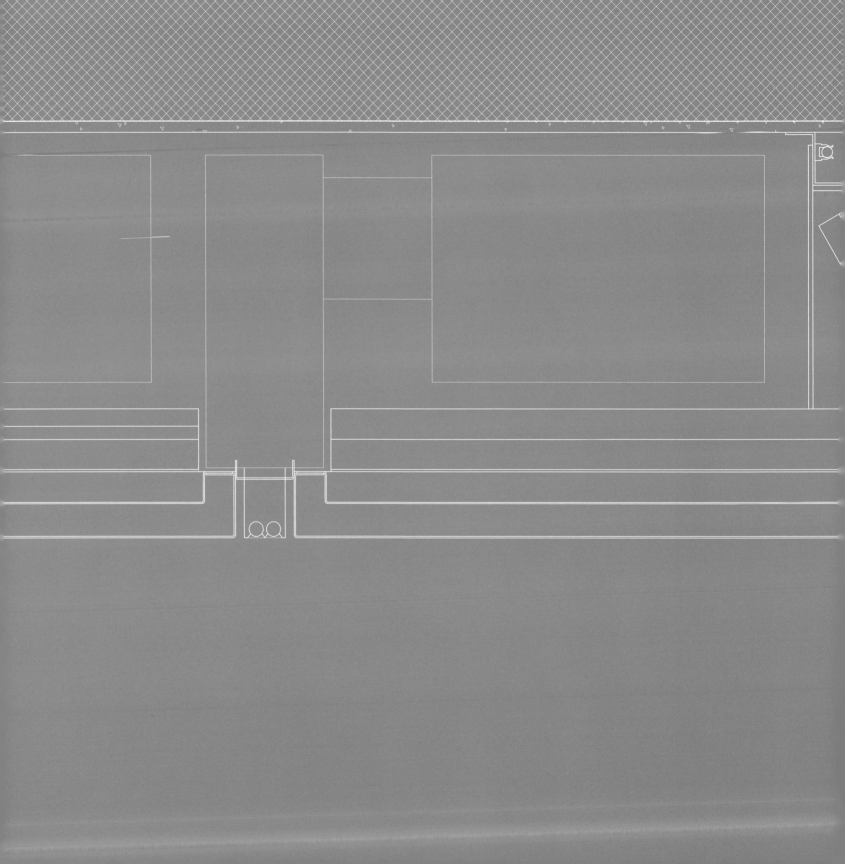

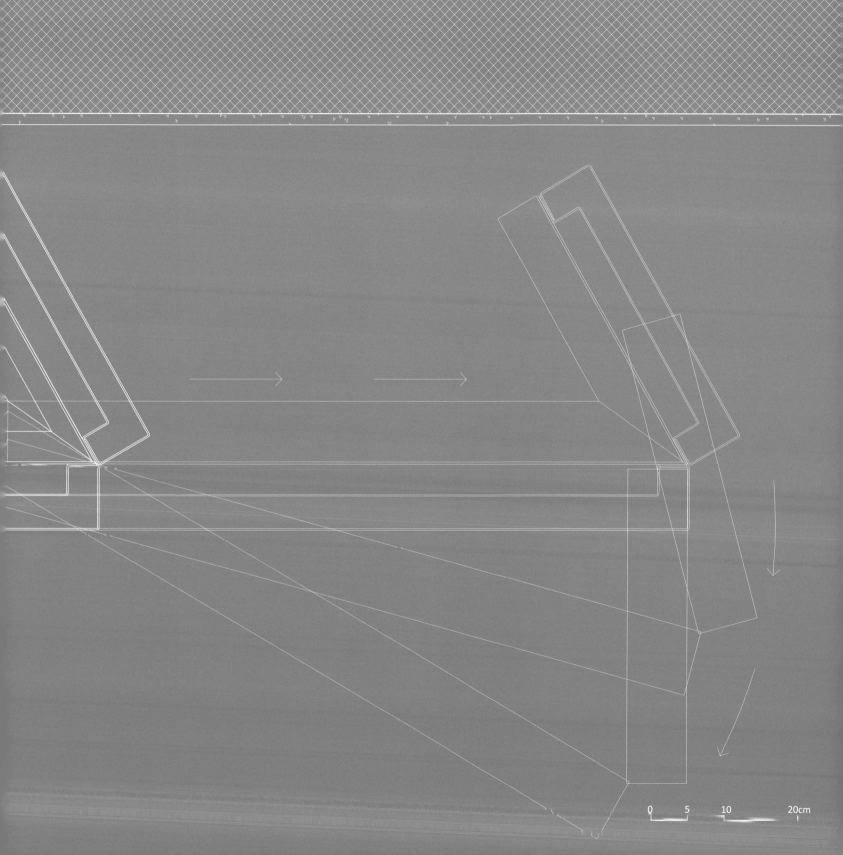

0   5   10   20cm

Open space office with Davide
Macullo's *Iscape* sketch

Pages 94-95
Open space office with Davide
Macullo's *Iscape* sketch

Pages 96-97
Meeting areas in the Campus
with art work by Tanja Roscic

Pages 98-99
Graphic led light design office
entrance doors

Pages 100-101
Left: Meeting room with art work
Staircase by Phyllida Barlow
Right: Circulation area with art work
Valley Drip Releaf by Sopheap Pitch

Pages 102-103
Left: Jansen communication office
Right: Office space with sculpture
Cubescape by Davide Macullo

Ikarus

Business Engineering
QUS Management

Boardroom
Art work *Stream Triangle*
by Haruhiko Sunagawa

Opposite page
Art work *Bent Mies*
by Robin Rhode

Boardroom table by Davide Macullo
Architects, view from below

0 10 20   50cm

Relation between internal
and external landscape
Above right: Art work
Flat Building M by Dong-Yeon Kim

Priska & Christoph Jansen

*Members of the Supervisory Board
and the Jansen Group Management Board*

Family values

Values help us choose what is right for us from the almost infinite number of possibilities. Values are therefore a little like signposts or roadside barriers. They have long-term validity and as a consequence are more binding than actual visions and objectives. In a changing environment, objectives are always having to be realigned or modified, but values endure and bring security and stability – for our customers and our employees.

We have been living by many of our values since the founding of our family firm around 90 years ago. Then, our grandfather, Josef Jansen, took ownership of a small workshop in Oberriet in St. Gallen in the Upper Rhine Valley. His focus was on the respect and appreciation of his employees, a healthy financial position and, above all, products in tune with the market.

Purposefully, he set about expanding the business step by step. A process continued by his sons Leo, Peter and Walter. They diversified into new applications and areas of business and launched the company internationally.

They gave us, Priska and Christoph, the opportunity to join a healthy and dynamic family-owned company. Today, we can develop and shape the company in its third generation of family ownership.

The original workforce of 20 has grown to 1,000. To the armoured steel pipes have been added steel tubes, steel profile systems, plastic pipes and a wide range of trade products. And the 40,000 Swiss francs annual turnover has reached 300 million. Much of what was then made by hand is now automated.

But through all these changes, Jansen has retained the same key values. We are still growing in massive steps by our own efforts. We have always reinvested a large part of the profits in the company. The investment we have made in recent years in our headquarters in Oberriet shows that we believe in the future of our Swiss industrial base.

But we also recognise that development is just as important as production. So while we have invested in state-of-the-art production systems and buildings, we have also created a space, in the form of the Jansen Campus, where our employees can interact and further develop in a dynamic environment.

And in the Jansen Campus we find many elements that remind us of our values: the high quality of the architecture and the activities within, the long-term vision of this investment, the development of refined detailed solutions and ultimately the respect and appreciation of our employees.

To develop a company over generations, it is not enough simply to copy the past. Changing conditions must be continuously judged against our strengths and values. Davide Macullo coined the phrase "we must understand" in this context. He sums up very beautifully where our main challenges lie – whether in the development of our company or in the planning of the Jansen Campus. We must understand what the needs of our customers, partners and employees are. And we must understand what opportunities we can exploit in demanding conditions. "We must understand" is therefore the precondition for every successful change.

This will allow us to hand over our family firm at some time in the future to a next generation. And allow them to find new solutions and take new paths – while continuing to preserve our proven values.

Pages 118-119
Study model with future extension

Pages 120-121
Sketch by Davide Macullo

Pages 122-123
Staircase suspended ceiling

Fact sheet

Davide Macullo Architects
Jansen Campus in Oberriet, SG,
Switzerland

Project name:
Jansen Campus
Site:
Oberriet, SG, Switzerland
Function:
Office building
Client:
Jansen AG
Start of project:
July 2008
Beginning of construction:
May 2010
End of construction:
May 2012
Certification:
Minergie standard

Plot area:
3,705 m²
Building footprint:
1,100 m²
Gross floor area:
3,300 m²
Gross floor area below ground:
900 m²
Gross floor area above ground:
2,400 m²
Volume:
15,800 m³
Floors:
1 basement, 4 upper floors

Materials
Primary structure:
Reinforced concrete

Outer lining
Facades:
Expanded metal mesh made from a titanium
zinc alloy (from the company Rheinzink),
prepatinated
Wind protection barrier
Windows:
Jansen VISS SG Structural Glazing
Sloped roofs:
Prepapinated zinc alloy
by Rheinzink
Flat roofs:
Prefabricated concrete panels,
gravel

Inner lining
Walls:
Plaster
Ceilings:
Plaster
Floor covering:
Parquet, natural stone

Building owner:
Jansen AG – Oberriet SG
Architect:
Davide Macullo
Davide Macullo Architects – Lugano TI
Project architect:
Lorenza Tallarini, Davide Macullo Architects
– Lugano TI

Design collaborators:
Ah Lom Kim, Aileen Forbes-Munnelly,
Karen Abernethy, Michele Alberio,
Samuela Pfund, Davide Macullo Architects
Landscape architect:
Davide Macullo Architects – Lugano TI
Interior designer:
Davide Macullo Architects – Lugano TI
Project management,
site supervision: Architekten: rlc AG
- Rheineck SG
Civil engineer:
Wälli AG Ingenieure – St. Gallen SG
Building engineer, acoustics:
Baumann Akustik und Bauphysik AG
- Dietfurt SG
HVAC, sanitary and electric
engineering and coordination:
Amstein und Walthert AG – St. Gallen SG
Lighting engineer:
Caduff Lichtplanung – Dietikon ZH
Facade design:
Fiorio Fassadentechnik GmbH
- Zuzwil SG
Door design:
Dileis – St. Gallen SG
Building contractors:
Gautschi AG – St. Margrethen SG,
Johann Loher AG – Montlingen SG,
Kühnis AG – Oberriet SG
Facade construction:
L + K Fassaden AG – St. Gallen SG
Sloped roofs:
Loher Spenglertechnik AG – Oberriet SG,
Rossi AG – Oberburen SG

Glazing / external doors:
Aepli Metallbau AG – Gossau SG
Interior doors:
Wehrli Metallbau AG – Wil SG
Floor covering parquet:
Parkett Bösch GmbH – Zürich ZH
Floor covering natural stone:
Urban Loher – Montlingen SG
Suspended ceilings:
Lüchinger Metallbau AG
– Kriessern SG
Kühnis metallplan – Montlingen SG
Light fittings:
Regent Beleuchtungskörper AG
– Zürich ZH
Audio, video:
Büro Tech Spirig AG – Berneck SG
Furniture:
Cappellini Spa – Meda I
Alias Spa – Grumello del Monte I
Sara SA – Tenero TI
Stoll Giroflex AG– Koblenz AG
Danese s.r.l. – Milano I
Custom furniture:
Frei Holzbau AG – Kriessern SG
Zomo-form – Au SG
Art advisor:
ART303 – Seoul KR
Printed material:
Kupka Werbeproduktion AG
– Montlingen SG
Horticulture:
Bucher AG – Widnau SG
Civil engineering, roads:
Hugo Dietsche AG   Kriessern SG

Sanitary installations:
Tiziani Haustechnik GmbH –
Montlingen SG
Adolf Hasler AG – Oberriet SG
Electrical equipment:
Kolb Elektro AG – Oberriet SG
RHV Elektrotechnik AG – Altstätten SG
HVAC:
Hälg &Co AG – St. Gallen SG

Buildings and projects

2013

Residential Complex
Rancate, Ticino
Floor Area 12,000 m²
Ongoing

House Refurbishment
Viganello, Switzerland
Floor Area 600 m²
Under Construction

Apartment Refurbishment
Lugano, Switzerland
Floor Area 220 m²
Under Construction

Penthouse Office
Refurbishment
Lugano, Switzerland
Floor Area 260 m²
Under Construction

House
Montagnola, Switzerland
Floor Area 270 m²
Ongoing

Rhyboot Workshop
Complex
Altstätten, Switzerland
Floor Area 4,700 m²
Competition

Extension to Historical
House
Milan, Italy
Floor Area 600 m²
Ongoing

National Theatre Balilla
Refurbishment
Milan, Italy
Floor Area 2,500 m²
Ongoing

"Café à porter" Take Away
Lugano, Switzerland
Floor Area 30 m²
Ongoing

Graphic Design for
a Greek Airline
Ongoing

2012

Swiss Embassy
Seoul, South Korea
Floor Area 780 m²
Competition

Library
Daegu, South Korea
Floor Area 1,500 m²
Competition

Apartment Refurbishment
Castagnola, Switzerland
Floor Area 100 m²
Ongoing

Traditional House
Refurbishment
Origlio, Switzerland
Floor Area 106 m²
Project

Two Seafront Villas
Patra, Greece
Floor Area 700 m²
Ongoing

House Refurbishment
Palm Beach, USA
Floor Area 400 m²
Built

Mondaine Watch
Stand for Baselworld 2013
Basel, Switzerland
Floor Area 200 m²
Ongoing

Huhu Dang Museum
Hwacheon, South Korea
Floor Area 2,000 m²
Ongoing

House
Preonzo, Switzerland
Floor Area 240 m²
Under Construction

Housing on Lake Lugano
Maroggia, Switzerland
Floor Area 2,700 m²
Under Construction

Office Building
Refurbishment
Athens, Greece
Floor Area 1,300 m²
Built

Jansen Office Building
Refurbishment
Oberriet, Switzerland
Floor Area 3,000 m²
Project

Three Villas
Chuncheon, South Korea
Floor Area 600 m²
Ongoing

Spa Club Bürgenstock
Resort
Bürgenstock, Switzerland
Floor Area 2,000 m²
Invited Competition

Apartment Refurbishment
Gstaad, Switzerland
Floor Area 300 m²
Ongoing

Hotel Sommerau
Chur, Switzerland
Floor Area 2,800 m²
Project

2011

AC Milan Stores Concept
for China Market
China
Floor Area 250 m²
Project

AET Headquarters
Bellinzona, Switzerland
Floor Area 2,000 m²
Competition

Apartment Complex H
Vimercate, Italy
Floor Area 5,400 m²
Ongoing

Apartment Complex
Caravaggio, Italy
Floor Area 5,000 m²
Competition

Contest Housing
Milan, Italy
Floor Area 5,000 m²
Competition

Cubescape Sculpture
for Marmi + Graniti Italia
Milan, Italy

Retirement Home
Samedan, Switzerland
Floor Area 14,700 m²
Competition

Greenline Fitness Centre
Rho, Italy
Floor Area 700 m²
Built

Hotel, Hot Springs
+ Wellness Centre
Beijing, China
Floor Area 70,000 m²
Invited Competition

House
Giornico, Switzerland
Floor Area 150 m²
Project

House in Savosa
Lugano, Switzerland
Floor Area 600 m²
Project

Jansen Spedition Hall
Oberriet, Switzerland
Floor Area 1,200 m²
Built

Industrial Masterplan
Carate Brianza, Italy
Floor Area 5,500 m²
Ongoing

Sales Centre
Tianjin, China
Floor Area 2,000 m²
Built

Sulbiate Auditorium
Vimercate, Italy
Floor Area 200 m²
Ongoing

USI/SUPSI Campus
Lugano, Switzerland
Floor Area 37,000 m²
Competition

2010

Apartment Building
Vimercate, Italy
Floor Area 1,200 m²
Under Construction

Area ex Motta Apartment
Building
Lissone, Italy
Floor Area 20,000 m²
Project

Area ex Ospedale
Masterplan
Vimercate, Italy
Floor Area 135,000 m²
Ongoing

Retirement Home
Giornico, Switzerland
Floor Area 5,000 m²
Competition

Dongxiang Headquarters
Beijing, China
Floor Area 85,000 m²
Invited Competition

Jeju Holiday House 1
Jeju Island, South Korea
Floor Area 150 m²
Project

Jeju Holiday House 2
Jeju Island, South Korea
Floor Area 150 m²
Project

House for Gianni
Vimercate, Italy
Floor Area 150 m²
Project

House
Santa Maria, Switzerland
Floor Area 120 m²
Project

House in Valaa
Lugano, Switzerland
Floor Area 600 m²
Ongoing

House
Vimodrone, Italy
Floor Area 250 m²
Ongoing

Meta Energia
Fiera di Milano
Milan, Italy
Floor Area 170 m²
Built

New Art Gallery
Maribor, Slovenia
Floor Area 17,000 m²
Competition

New Robbiati Factory
+ Offices
Bernareggio, Italy
Floor Area 3,600 m²
Under Construction

Nursery School
Comano, Switzerland
Floor Area 2,000 m²
Competition

Ospedale Vimercate
Interiors
Vimercate, Italy
Floor Area 30,000 m²
Built

Palazzo della Regione
Lombardia Interiors
Milan, Italy
Floor Area 5,000 m²
Competition - 1st Prize

Retail + Apartments Scheme
Vimodrone, Italy
Floor Area 300 m²
Project

Waterfront Clubhouse
Tianjin, China
Floor Area 7,000 m²
Invited Competition

Zollverein School of Design
Essen, Germany
Floor Area 24,000 m²
Invited Competition

2009

Apartment Building
Castagnola, Switzerland
Floor Area 3,500 m²
Project

Apartment Building
Monza, Italy
Floor Area 4,200 m²
Ongoing

Apartment Building La Pesa
Rovagnate, Italy
Floor Area 2,800 m²
Project

Apartment Building
Cadro, Switzerland
Floor Area 750 m²
Project

Architecture + Design
Museum
Oslo, Norway
Floor Area 36,000 m²
Competition

Art Fund Pavillion
London, UK
Floor Area 120 m²
Competition

Calderwood Housing
Competition
Scotland, UK
Floor Area 13,600 m²
Competition - Awarded

Civic Hall Competition
Echandens, Switzerland
Floor Area 2,300 m²
Competition

Expo 2012 Competition
Yeosu, South Korea
Floor Area 8,000 m²
Competition

Hair + Beauty Studio
Athens, Greece
Floor Area 300 m²
Project

House in Canobbio
Lugano, Switzerland
Floor Area 230 m²
Built

House
Lumino, Switzerland
Floor Area 221 m²
Built

Lee Wal Chong House
Museum
Jeju Island, South Korea
Floor Area 1,332 m²
Built

Medical Spa Maffeo
Vimercate, Italy
Floor Area 2,000 m²
Under Construction

Naturmuseum Competition
St. Gallen, Switzerland
Floor Area 5,500 m²
Competition

Nursery School Competition
Taverne, Switzerland
Floor Area 1,600 m²
Competition

Pier Museum Competition
Miami, USA
Floor Area 1,800 m²
Competition

Refurbishment of a House
Rossa, Switzerland
Floor Area 100 m²
Under Construction

Seafront House
Heraklion, Greece
Floor Area 400 m²
Under Construction

Three Houses
Athens, Greece
Floor Area 750 m²
Built

Unesco Museum
Naters, Switzerland
Floor Area 13,000 m²
Competition

Private Spa + Sauna
Oberriet, Switzerland
Floor Area 23 m²
Built

2008

House
Athens, Greece
Floor Area 400 m²
Project

Apartment Building
Abu Dhabi, UAE
Floor Area 15,000 m²
Invited Competition

Commercial Building
Acero Rosso
Bernareggio, Italy
Floor Area 2,800 m²
Built

Holiday House
Taormina, Italy
Floor Area 450 m²
Under Construction

Hotel
Vimercate, Italy
Floor Area 10,000 m²
Ongoing

House
Guachon, South Korea
Floor Area 270 m²
Project

House
Mendrisio, Switzerland
Floor Area 200 m²
Project

House
Pilio, Greece
Floor Area 450 m²
Project

Kim Chan Wan House
Seoul, South Korea
Floor Area 540 m²
Project

Lighting Design Pentalight
Italy

Loft
Athens, Greece
Floor Area 150 m²
Built

Magok Waterfront
Magok, South Korea
Competition

Museum of Ethnography
Geneva, Switzerland
Floor Area 6,000 m²
Competition

New Factory Elevations
Busnago, Italy
Floor Area 5,000 m²
Ongoing

Office Building
Athens, Greece
Floor Area 800 m²
Project

Country House
Refurbishment
Uzes, France
Site Area 20,000 m²
Built

Refurbishment
of Hotel Suites
in Grand Resort Lagonissi
Athens, Greece
Floor Area 1,000 m²
Built

Talassotherapy Centre
Spotorno, Italy
Floor Area 2,900 m²
Under Construction

Villas at Golf Cub
Villa Paradiso
Trezzo d'Adda, Italy
Floor Area 4,500 m²
Project

Yachting Club Villas -
Elounda Beach Resort
Crete, Greece
Floor Area 15,500 m²
Built

2007

Barbour Apartment
Complex
Vimercate, Italy
Floor Area 15,000 m²
Ongoing

Conference Centre
at Grand Resort Lagonissi
Athens, Greece
Floor Area 15,000 m²
Ongoing

Graphic Design
for Yamamay
Italy
Project

House in Carabbia
Lugano, Switzerland
Floor Area 169 m²
Built

House
Caprino, Switzerland
Floor Area 200 m²
Project

House in Rio Patra I
Rio Patra, Greece
Floor Area 700 m²
Project

House in Rio Patra II
Rio Patra, Greece
Floor Area 400 m²
Project

Housing
Bernareggio, Italy
Floor Area 2,400 m²
Project

Colombo Factory Offices
Milan, Italy
Floor Area 220 m²
Project

Refurbishment of Monastery
San Lorenzo into Hotel
Vimercate, Italy
Floor Area 2,200 m2
Under Construction

Urban Regeneration
of Lumino Centre
Lumino, Switzerland
Site Area 10,000 m²
Invited Competition

Retail Centre and
Residences Magnetti
Cisano Bergamasco, Italy
Floor Area 50,000 m²
Competition

Row Housing
Oreno, Italy
Floor Area 4,000 m²
Ongoing

Terrace Housing
Besazio, Switzerland
Floor Area 2,100 m²
Project

2006

Apartment Building
Cornate d'Adda, Italy
Floor Area 2,000 m²
Under Construction

Club House at Golf Club
Villa Paradiso
Trezzo d'Adda, Italy
Floor Area 400 m²
Project

Commercial Building
Pioppo Nero
Bernareggio, Italy
Floor Area 1,100 m²
Built

Jeongok Prehistory Museum
Gyeonggi-do, South Korea
Floor Area 10,000 m²
Competition

House
Ticino, Switzerland
Floor Area 232 m²
Built

House in Comano
Lugano, Switzerland
Floor Area 200 m²
Built

House
Agno, Switzerland
Floor Area 200 m²
Project

House
Agno, Switzerland
Floor Area 250 m²
Project

Jewellery Design
with Jacqueline Rabun
London, UK
Project

Offices Refurbishment
Geneva, Switzerland
Floor Area 350 m²
Project

House Refurbishment
Giubiasco, Switzerland
Floor Area 350 m²
Built

Liberty Villa Refurbishment
Bellinzona, Switzerland
Floor Area 350 m²
Built

Spa and Wellness Facilities
at Elounda Beach Resort
Crete, Greece
Floor Area 1,500 m²
Built

Urban Development
Housing
Bernareggio, Italy
Floor Area 11,000 m2
Project

2005

Abu Dhabi International
Competition
Abu Dhabi, UAE
Floor Area 40,000 m²
Invited Competition

Alzheimer Clinic
Athens, Greece
Floor Area 40,000 m²
Project

Alzheimer Clinic Il Ronco
in Casasco
Como, Italy
Floor Area 4,500 m²
Competition - 1st Prize

Apartment Building
Cari, Switzerland
Floor Area 1,600 m²
Project

House Extension
Gingins, Switzerland
Floor Area 250 m²
Project

House Extension
and Noise Protection
Piano di Magadino,
Switzerland
Floor Area 220 m²
Project

JR Jewellery Shop
London, UK
Floor Area 200 m²
Project

Renovation La Ticinella
Stabio, Switzerland
Floor Area 300 m²
Project

Town Houses
and Apartments
Apeldoorn, Netherlands
Floor Area 40,000 m²
Project

Villas at Grand Resort
Lagonissi
Athens, Greece
Floor Area 27,000 m²
Project

2004

Apartment
Lugano, Switzerland
Floor Area 100 m²
Built

Apartment Building
Vimercate, Italy
Floor Area 1,300 m²
Under Construction

Apartment Building
Davesco, Switzerland
Floor Area 1,000 m²
Project

Apartment Building
Lugano, Switzerland
Floor Area 3,200 m²
Project

Atrium for Union
of Journalists
Athens, Greece
Floor Area 50 m²
Built

Campus of the Swiss
Italian University
Lugano, Switzerland
Floor Area 5,200 m²
Competition

House in Gorduno
Bellinzona, Switzerland
Floor Area 203 m²
Built

House in Salorino
Mendrisio, Switzerland
Floor Area 180 m²
Built

House for Archibald the Dog
Lugano, Switzerland
Floor Area 2 m²
Built

Industrial Convertion
for Lofts
Carate Brianza, Italy
Floor Area 10,000 m²
Project

Municipal Offices
Boxmer, Netherlands
Floor Area 4,800 m²
Invited Competition

Panoramic Restaurant and
Lounge Amemoni
Nauplia, Greece
Floor Area 800 m²
Project

Renovation and Extension
Hotel Galaxy
Heraklion, Greece
Floor Area 3,000 m²
Project

2003

Apartment
Lugano, Switzerland
Floor Area 150 m²
Project

Bio-Ecological
Buildings Aler
Varese, Italy
Floor Area 11,000 m²
Competition

House
Biasca, Switzerland
Floor Area 200 m²
Project

Public Schools and
Municipal Offices
Sonvico, Switzerland
Floor Area 1,800 m²
Competition

2002

Exhibition Design
for Tragedy
Zurich, Switzerland
Floor Area 1,200 m²
Built

Police Headquarters
Giubiasco, Switzerland
Floor Area 3,600 m²
Competition - Awarded

Hotel Xenia
Nauplia, Greece
Floor Area 7,000 m²
Ongoing

House
Muzzano, Switzerland
Floor Area 379 m²
Built

House
Olsberg, Switzerland
Floor Area 300 m²
Project

House
Dino, Switzerland
Floor Area 220 m²
Project

House Passeri
Bioggio, Switzerland
Floor Area 200 m²
Project

House Sukow
Bioggio, Switzerland
Floor Area 200 m²
Project

New Office Spaces
at Migros Museum
Zurich, Switzerland
Floor Area 300 m²
Project

Penthouse
Castagnola, Switzerland
Floor Area 100 m²
Built

Urban Planning
Muzzano, Switzerland
Floor Area 10,000 m²
Competition - Awarded
Project

2001

Apartment
Lugano, Switzerland
Floor Area 95 m²
Built

Exhibit-Stand for
Books Artinprogress
- Fine Arts Unternehmen
Berlin, Germany
Built

House
Preonzo, Switzerland
Floor Area 220 m²
Project

2000

Loft
Lugano, Switzerland
Floor Area 300 m²
Built

Twin Houses Giotto
Biasca, Switzerland
Floor Area 360 m²
Project

1999

Municipal House
Pregassona, Switzerland
Floor Area 3,600 m²
Competition

Refuge in the Alps
in the Cristallina Peaks
Switzerland
Floor Area 2,000 m²
Competition

Residential and Commercial
Building
Ochsenhausen, Germany
Floor Area 3,600 m²
Project

1998

Pedestrian Bridge
on the River
Lodrino, Switzerland
Built

House Refurbishment
Lugano, Switzerland
Floor Area 300 m²
Built

Weekend House
Rossa, Switzerland
Floor Area 80 m²
Built

1997

Residential Quarter
Bergamo, Italy
Floor Area 7,000 m²
Competition

1996

Public Buildings
and Infrastructures
San Bernardino,
Switzerland
Floor Area 2,800 m²
Competition

Public Square
Ludiano, Switzerland
Floor Area 400 m²
Project

1995

Fashion Boutique
Seoul, South Korea
Floor Area 500 m²
Built

House Refurbishment
Gorduno, Switzerland
Floor Area 400 m²
Built

Municipal House
Refurbishment
Acquarossa, Switzerland
Floor Area 250 m²
Project

Row-houses, Factory
and Garage
Malvaglia, Switzerland
Floor Area 300 m²
Project

European Student Housing
Pavia, Italy
Floor Area 4,000 m²
Competition

1994

Residential and Commercial
Building "Piano Forte"
Lugano, Switzerland
Floor Area 7,000 m²
Project

1992

House
Mendrisio, Switzerland
Floor Area 250 m²
Project

Municipal House
Refurbishment
Semione, Switzerland
Floor Area 150 m²
Built

Willkommen

Publications

2013

Architectural Facade, Hong Kong Polytechnic International Publishing Co., Ltd., China.
"Regardez la nouvelle façade attrayante avec métal étiré", *Bâtitech*, no.1/2, USTSC, Switzerland.
"Un toit difficile avec de grandes longueurs couvert à double agrafage en Rheinzink", *Bâtitech*, no.3, USTSC, Switzerland.
"Building a Vision", *Building Giants*, ABS Publication, February, India.
"Kristall aus Oberriet", *Gebäudehülle*, no. 02, Assoc. des Entreprises l'Enveloppe des Edifices, Switzerland
"Not to be a Lonely Artist", *Real Home*, The Beijing News, February, China.

2012

100XN Architecture Shape and Skin, 2012 Edition, Hong Kong Architecture Science Press, Hong Kong.
"Schulungszentrum in Oberriet", *AIT*, no. 9, Verlagsanstalt Alexander Koch GmbH, September, Germany.
"Jansen Campus", *Architecture + Detail*, no. 5, Dalian University of Technology Press, China.
"Cover Story Jansen Campus", *Architecture and Culture*, no. 374, ANC Book, July, South Korea.
"Cover Story Jansen Campus", *Architecture World*, no. 206, Archiworld

PA, July, South Korea.
"Gebaute Visionen", *Architektur + Technik*, Sonderausgabe Fassaden, B+L Verlags AG, Switzerland.
"Produkt am Bau", *Architektur + Technik*, no. 1, B+L Verlags AG, Switzerland.
"Jansen Campus", *Architektur Heute*, no. 4, Switzerland.
"Die neue Fassade vom Campus Jansen mit Rheinzink", *Bauflash*, no. 11, Verlag Laupper, Switzerland.
"Dach und Fassade am neuen Campus Jansen in Oberriet", *Bauen Heute*, no. 10, D+D Verlag, Switzerland.
"Jansen Campus", *Bau Info*, no. 7, Herausgeberin und Verlag, Switzerland.
"Blick auf die Neue", *Bau Info*, no. 10, Herausgeberin und Verlag, Switzerland.
"Das anspruchsvolle Dach", *Bau Info*, no. 12, Herausgeberin und Verlag, Switzerland.
"Office Architecture", *Beyond*, no. 14, Tang Art Design + Information Group, Hong Kong.
Building Skin, Hong Kong Polytechnic International Publishing Co. Ltd, China.
CAD Collective Drawings of Architectural Design Detail, ThinkArchit Group, Huazhong University of Science and Technology Press, China.
"Gebaute Visionen",

Fassade Façade, no. 3, szff/csff, Switzerland.
Fine and Pure Modern Interior Design, Open & Huazhong University of Science and Technology Press, China.
Global Architecture Studio, Rihan Technology, Beijing, China.
Headquarters Base, Hi-Design International Publishing, Hong Kong.
Hotel Decor, Designer Books, Hong Kong.
"Grosse Flachen, beschwingt, lebendig und voller raffinierter Leichtigkeit", *HK-Gebäudetechnik*, no.11, AZ Fachverlage AG, Switzerland.
"Aspiring to the Classics", *Interior Design*, November, USA.
"Jansen Campus: Building a Vision", *Interior Magazine*, no. 229, October, Taiwan.
"Celebrity of IW: Davide Macullo Architects Interior World", *Archiworld*, no. 108, July, South Korea.
"Cover Story Building a Vision", *International New Architecture*, no. 12, Ifengspace Shanghai, China.
"Von der Vision zur Hülle", *Klempner Magazin*, no. 6, Verlag Rudolf Müller, Germany.
Leisure Hours, Restaurant + Spa Design, DesignerBooks, Hong Kong.

"Metall", *SMU*, July, Switzerland.
"Floating above the Sea at Crete", *Objekt International*, no. 56, Fonk Publications, Holland.
"Yachting Club Villas at Elounda Beach, Crete", *Objekt Russia*, no. 12, Hans Fonk Publications, Moscow, Russia.
"Jansen Campus", *Salon*, no. 11, CJSC Ukrainian Publishing House Ukraine, Ukraine.
Swissmadeinitaly. Davide Macullo Architects, Yao Jing (Ed.), Ifengspace, China.
"Jansen Campus", *Touch Decor*, no. 28, M+A Services, July-October, Lebanon.
Vues du Zinc, no. 6, VMZinc, October, Switzerland.
"Jansen Campus", *Workshop*, no. 07, Choi Gallery Publication, California + Shanghai.
World Architecture 1, Madison Series, China.

2011

150 + Residences of the World, ThinkArchit Group, China.
200 Houses, M. Cleary (Ed.), Images Publishing, Australia.
"The State of Contemporary Korean Architecture", *Architecture & Culture*, no. 361, A&C Publishing, June, South Korea.
A Grand Collection

of Magnificent Villas,
Ifengspace, China.
A Prize Exposynergy
Miodino premia
l'architettura, Exposyenrgy,
Italy.
Architecture Highlights 3,
ShangLin A&C Limited,
Hong Kong, China.
Architetture per un
territorio sostenibile,
Marcello Balzani + Nicola
Marzot, Skira, Italy.
Arch-Manual 4, AADCU
Program, Ifengspace,
China.
Artwork: Restaurant &
Hotel Design, Ifengspace,
China.
Betonprisma, no. 92,
Informations Zentrum
Beton GmbH, July,
Germany.
Detail in Architetuur,
Sdu Uitgevers, February,
Nederlands.
Die Besten
Einfamilienhauser, H.
Rauterberg + B. Hintze,
Callwey, Germany.
"Shifting Planes", Inside
Outside, no. 308, Business
India Publications,
February, India.
"Un monolithe strict
et linéaire", Maisons
et Ambiances, no. 3,
Editions Etzel, May-June,
Switzerland.
"La Casa en Lumino
Suiza", En Blanco, no. 6,
General de Ediciones de
Arquitectura, Spain.
"The Peaceful Garden.
Vimercate Hospital",
Interior Public Space,
Dalian University of

Technology Press, August,
China.
"Une architecture
géométrique comme
interface avec le passé",
Villas, no. 81, Eder SA,
February, Belgium.
Villas of the World, Boyuan
Int'l Press Co. Ltd., China.
Upper Class Club, Design
Vision, Fujian Science and
Technology Publishing
House, China.
"Cleantech Switzerland
and Macullo Success
Story", Cleantech, August,
Switzerland.
"Neubau Jansen Campus",
Panorama, no. 10+11,
Switzerland.

2010
"Yacht Club Villas at
Elounda Beach Resort",
Architecture & Culture,
no. 344, A&C Publishing,
January, South Korea.
"House in Canobbio",
Archiworld, no. 176,
January, South Korea.
"Auf der Sonnenseite des
Lebens", Baumetall, no. 25,
TFV Fachverlag, February,
Germany.
"House in Lumino,
Switzerland", Beton. TKS,
no. 6, SVB, December,
Czech Republic.
"House in Lumino",
Country Housing + Culture,
no. 142, December, South
Korea.
"Blocco alla ticinese",
Costruire, no. 321, Editrice
Abitare Segesta, February,
Italy.
"House in Canobbio",

Details, no. 19, A&C
Publishing, January, South
Korea.
"Audaz, con naturalidad",
Espacio & Confort, no.
75, Klima Visual, June,
Argentina.
"House in Lumino", Hise,
House of the World, no. 59,
Zavod Big, May, Slovenia.
"House in Lumino", Interior
World, no. 83, Archiworld,
February, South Korea.
IQD Inside Quality Design,
no. 15, Verbus Edtrice, July-
September, Italy.
"Jansen baut Campus,
mit Schüler Mario Bottas",
Der Rheintaler, 30 April,
Switzerland.
"Cizgiden gercege",
Konsept Projeler,
September, Turkey.
"A betondoboz inkább a
hegyek szikláival, mint a
környez" házak stilusával
van összefüggésben",
Metszet, no. 1, Artifex
Kiado, January-February,
Hungary.
"Bauen mit
Fingerspitzengefühl",
Oberes Rheintal, 31 May,
Switzerland.
"House in Canobbio",
"House in Lumino", Omni
Housing, no. 8, Archiworld,
South Korea.
"Casa a Lumino, Alpi
svizzere", Ottagono, no.
227, Editrice Compositori,
February, Italy.
Marcello Balzani, Progetto
per l'abitare, Maggioli, Italy.
"Innovativer Monolith mit
Bezug zur Tradition", Raum
und Wohnen, no. 6-7,

Etzel-Verlag AG, July-
August, Switzerland.
"Wir sind für die Zukunft
gerüstet", Rheinalische
Volkszeitung, 27 May,
Switzerland.
"Tre progetti per il futuro
della città", Giornale di
Vimercate, 20 April, Italy.
"Jansen baut 'Campus',
mit Schüler Mario Bottas",
Der Rheintaler, 30 April,
Switzerland.

2009
"Carabbia House",
"Comano House", "Ticino
House", 100 Country
Houses, Beth Browne,
Images Publishing,
Australia.
"Casa d'abitazione rivestita
in metallo", Archi, no. 1,
SIA, Switzerland.
"House in Carabbia",
"House in Comano",
Details, no. 13, A&C
Publishing, January,
South Korea.
"Ein schiff wird...",
Architektur & Technik, B+L
Verlags AG, November,
Switzerland.
"Nella Thala Spa
dell'Elounda Beach Hotel
& Villas", Area Wellness,
no. 38, Headmaster
International Srl, July-
August, Italy.
"Giornico", Baubiologie,
no. 1, Switzerland.
"The Dinamic Duo",
Big Fish, Proto Thema
Newspapers, May, Greece.
"Case creative – fantasia
therapy", Casaviva, no. 2,
Mondadori, February, Italy.

"House in Lumino", *Details*, no. 18, A&C Publishing, December, South Korea.
"The Ultimate Expression of Glamorous, Ultra-modern Hotel Living", *Harpers' Bazaar*, Hearst Communications, United Kingdom.
IQD Inside Quality Design, no. 14, Verbus Editrice, Italy.
"TECU Architecture Award 2007", *KME*, KME Group, Germany.
"Pool House Uzes - France", *Monitor*, no. 55, mode…information, August, Italy.
"La forma del sentir", *Supplemento Home*, Argentina.
"Ticino House", *The Architectural Review*, Emap Inform, November, United Kingdom.
"Living in a Swiss Eco-house", *World Radio Switzerland*, interview, March, Switzerland.
"Comprensione del paesaggio", *Ottagono*, no. 226, Editrice Compositori, December, Italy.

2008
"House in Ticino, Switzerland", *Architecture & Detail*, Metal Tectonic, August, China.
"KME/TECU Architecture Award 2007", *Architektur Aktuell - The Art of Building*, no. 336, Springer Verlag, March, Austria.
"Edles Metall", *Fassaden - Architectur & Technik*, Sonderausgabe 2008, Frener & Reifer Schweiz GmbH, Switzerland.
"Architect of the Month: Davide Macullo", *Archiworld*, no. 162, Archiworld, Seoul, South Korea.
"Paesaggio privato", *Costruire*, no. 299, Abitare Segesta, April, Italy.
House with a View. Residential Mountain Architecture, Images Publishing, Australia.
"House in Comano", *Interior Architecture of China*, April-October, China.
"Casa a Carabbia, Canton Ticino", *L'Arca*, no. 235, L'Arca Editore, April, Italy.
"Casa in Ticino", *L'Architettura Naturale*, no. 40-41, Edicom, September-December, Italy.
"Vivienda en Ticino", *Metalocus*, no. 23, Metalocus, November, Spain.
"Single-family House Carabbia, Switzerland", *Monitor*, no. 49, Mode… Information, March, Russia.
"Contract Industry", *Ottagono*, no. 214, Editrice Compositori, October, Italy.
"House in Ticino", *Plan. The Art of Architecture and Design*, no. 7, July-August, Ireland.
Urban Style, Evergreen, Germany.

2007
"Maison à Comano", "Maison à Gorduno", "Loft à Castagnola", *Architecture Méditerranéenne*, no. 65, Edition R.K, December, France.
"Davide Macullo", *Architectura*, no. 59, Q-group Project, November, Romania.
"Geheimnisvoller Wohnbetonkubus", *Fokus Immobilien*, no. 3, Home & Business, April, Austria.
"Frammenti moderni", *Frames*, no. 125, Faenza Editrice, December, Italy.
"Grecia, avventura deluxe", *Grazia*, no. 27, July, Italy.
"I balsami di Venere", *Grecia. I Viaggi del Sole*, no. 7, Rizzoli Publishing Italia, July, Italy.
La Casa. Casa di Vacanza, no. 13, Federico Motta Editore, Italy.
"Davide Macullo", *La Vie d'Or*, no. 5, May, South Korea.
Progettare con il legno, Maggioli Editore, Italy.
Wallpaper Magazine, no. 101, Wallpaper, August, UK.

2006
Architecture in Switzerland, Taschen, Germany.
"Heaven on Earth", *Harper's Bazaar*, no. 11, Hearst Communications, United Kingdom.
M2. Minimum Space Maximum Living, Images Publishing, Australia.

2005
Beton 05, Cem-Suisse, Switzerland.
"Il paesaggio dentro", *Ottagono*, no. 177, Editrice Compositori, February, Italy.
"Casa unifamiliare", "Casa a Gorduno", *Young European Architects*, Clean Edizioni, Italy.

2004
Bagni, Federico Motta Editore, Italy.
"Vivere nel paesaggio", *Excellent*, no. 1, Cera L'H, November-December, Italy.
"Una costruzione di luce", *Frames*, no. 108, Faenza Editrice, February-March, Italy.
"Prestazioni ambientali di una serra", *Installatore*, no. 1, Fabio Sacchi, May, Switzerland.
"Un volume fortificato", *Ottagono*, no. 173, Editrice Compositori, September, Italy.
"Casa a Muzzano", "Casa a Gorduno", *Progetti di architettura bioecologica*, Maggioli Editore, Italy.
"Casa di vacanza a Rossa 1998, 47 mq", *Spazi minimi*, Federico Motta Editore, Italy.
"Wohnhaus in Muzzano", *Tessin Architektur*, Deutsche Verlags-Anstalt GmbH, Germany.

2003
"Prestazioni ambientali di una serra all'insegna del risparmio energetico", *ABCD*, no. 12, Edimet, December, Italy.
Case nel mondo, Federico Motta Editore, Italy.

Acknowledgements

One of the main purposes of this publication is to honour the commitment of all those who contributed to this extraordinary project and to recognise their collective efforts in the realisation of the Jansen Campus.

From the beginning, there was a genuine sense of teamwork, a spirit encouraged by an enlightened client and also a sense that each individual had the potential to gain and grow throughout project. There was a relentless pursuit of excellence in discovering and applying the latest and best construction technologies available and on site, the constant and spontaneous advice and suggestions of the engineers, workers and consultants created an atmosphere of appreciation and collective learning. The development and construction of the project created a special sentiment, one that will remain with those who worked on it throughout the rest of their careers. The significance of this project lies not only with its built form but in how hierarchies were broken down, ensuring everyone was afforded a sense of being indispensable through the attention to detail and the passion to do something well.

Biographical notes

Gabriele Cappellato, born in Padua, graduated from the Istituto Universitario di Architettura di Venezia (IUAV) in 1978 and completed his doctorate there in architectural design in 1984. He has collaborated with various Italian and international architecture firms and he is also currently completing some important architectural projects in Padua. He has been the editor of *Parametro* and *Ottagono* magazines and is currently editor of *Opera Progetto*. He has been a lecturer in various universities including the Faculty of Architecture of Ferrara and the Politecnico of Milan. He collaborated in 1994 with Mario Botta in the founding of the Academy of Architecture in Mendrisio, Switzerland. Since 1995, he has been professor of design, Dean of Students and responsible for the Bachelor degree at the Academy of Architecture of Mendrisio.

Kuno Bont was born and grew up in Oberriet. His favourite subjects as a film-maker, author and journalist are the people of the Rheintal. He represented the civil interests of the Rheintal population for many years as a representative on the cantonal great council and the local council. Today he lives in Werdenberg, a famous town dating from the Middle Ages, and produces films, musicals and plays. Kuno Bont received the Culture Prize of the Canton of St. Gallen, the Rheintal and the Buchs District Council for his services to culture and was awarded the East Switzerland Radio and Television Prize in 2000 for his documentary film *Die Rheinholzer* (*The Rhine Lumberjacks*).

Davide Macullo (born in Giornico, Switzerland, 1965) is a Swiss architect, living and working in Lugano, Switzerland. Previous to opening his own atelier, he was international project architect for Mario Botta for 20 years. Today his studio brings together an interdisciplinary group of professionals based in Switzerland, Italy, Greece, South Korea, China and India. The ethos of the studio is one of "drawing from context" and the various contributions promote a dialogue between the specificity of the project and the universality of the contexts. Current projects include several houses in the Swiss Alps, three beachfront properties in Greece, hotels in Nafplion and Lagonissi, Greece, a house and museum on Jeju island, Korea and a dozen residential, commercial and masterplan projects in Milan. The work of the studio has been published and acclaimed widely both at home and abroad.

Sophia Hyoseon Kim (born in Seoul, South Korea, 1967) studied German literature, art management and art history, receiving a diploma in art management and a masters in art history from the University of Paris-1. She spent seven years with the Galerie Denise René in Paris and has been the director of Gana Art Centre in Seoul. She founded her art consulting company in 2005 and has been responsible for the Woongjin Group Collection in Korea (2006-2009). She is currently an art advisor based in Seoul and works internationally in Europe and the USA. Her scope of work includes organising exhibitions, advising on collections, corporate art advisory and marketing service, art market research analysis and valuation, artist management and collaborating on architectural projects.

Pages 142-143
iew of the Rheintal region (winter)